MASTERS AT WORK

MASTERS AT WORK

BECOMING A VETERINARIAN

BORIS KACHKA

SIMON & SCHUSTER

New York   London   Toronto   Sydney   New Delhi

Simon & Schuster
1230 Avenue of the Americas
New York, NY 10020

First Simon & Schuster hardcover edition April 2019

SIMON & SCHUSTER and colophon are registered trademarks
of Simon & Schuster, Inc.

For information about special discounts for bulk purchases,
please contact Simon & Schuster Special Sales at 1-866-506-1949
or business@simonandschuster.com.

The Simon & Schuster Speakers Bureau can bring authors to your
live event. For more information or to book an event contact the
Simon & Schuster Speakers Bureau at 1-866-248-3049
or visit our website at www.simonspeakers.com.

Manufactured in the United States of America

1   3   5   7   9   10   8   6   4   2

Library of Congress Cataloging-in-Publication Data is available.

ISBN 978-1-5011-5946-6
ISBN 978-1-5011-5948-0 (ebook)

For my sister, Robin Kachka, DVM

CONTENTS

BECOMING
A
VETERINARIAN

INTRODUCTION

Elisha Frye was fresh out of Cornell veterinary school, a week into her job at a remote mixed-animal practice in rural Western New York, when her supervisor decided it was time for the rookie to get her hands dirty. Well into their overnight shift, a Mennonite farmer brought in a very pregnant and stoic seven-year-old golden retriever, an over-the-hill breeding dog whose litter wouldn't come out. A C-section was a fairly routine procedure, but not for Frye, who'd never performed one before, and not for the dog, Sandy, whose condition was worse than it looked.

Frye made a short incision into the dog's belly, and the first thing she saw was a puppy. The shocked young vet assumed she'd made the possibly fatal mistake of slitting the dog's uterus. But she quickly concluded the uterus must have ruptured on its own. Three other puppies were floating around in the abdomen, putting Sandy in grave danger of infection. Momentarily panicked, Frye started pulling on what she thought was a uterine horn—a tube ending in an ovary—but turned out to be the colon. "Extend your incision," her superior advised in a calm tone. "Get the anatomy straight." Frye found the ruptured horn, pulled out more puppies—eight in total—and spayed the poor overtaxed mother.

It was close to midnight by the time Sandy woke up from anesthesia. Leaving her in her cage overnight, Frye went home wondering if her first surgical patient would be alive in the morning. She hadn't had time to run the usual preoperative tests, and between blood loss and the risk of infection, there was no way of predicting whether she'd recover. Frye felt she was abandoning Sandy, but she had no choice. The following morning she rushed back and found Sandy energetically wagging her tail, just as she had when she'd first come in. "She recovered like a champ," says Frye, giving the retriever all the credit for her own quick, lifesaving work.

Eight years after the surgery, I visited the lakeside cabin Frye shares with her husband, Chris, a vet she met at Cornell; their baby daughter, Seneca; a one-eyed cat named Mr. Winks; and a surprisingly agile fifteen-year-old golden retriever—four years past the breed's average lifespan—who greeted me at the door with that same energetic wag of her tail.

The Fryes adopted Sandy two weeks after her surgery. At the urging of her boss and with Chris's wary consent ("as long as she's potty-trained," which Sandy was, more or less), Elisha paid the Mennonite farmer $30 to take the ex-breeding dog off his hands. Both Fryes knew there was still plenty of work to do—half a lifetime of care. Dogs spayed late in life are at very high risk of mammary cancer, so Elisha removed and biopsied two nipples, which tested negative. In the ensuing years it was Chris's particular set of skills that gave Sandy her second life. In 2016, Chris finished Cornell's first residency in animal sports medicine and rehab, which focuses partly on geriatric fitness. The leading vet school's brand-new department is as specialized as Elisha's practice is general; Chris is laser focused on dogs' muscles and nervous systems, while Elisha toggles between cow pregnancy checks, cat emergencies, goat tumors, and the occasional ailing snake.

Showing me around her current workplace, a ten-doctor mixed-animal practice in Cortland, New York, Elisha shows off a new X-ray machine and, suspended high above, the backlit film of a healthy dog femur. It's Sandy's hindquarters, and Frye likes to place it side-by-side with the X-rays of arthritic dogs to show owners the effects of a condition that Sandy has somehow evaded. Having eaten well and exercised her whole life, often tagging along on the Fryes' hikes and snowshoe outings and horseback rides, Sandy has defied all expectations for her age and breed. "It's crazy that she's alive, considering everything," says Frye—

never mind fully mobile (if quite deaf). "She's just this kind of miracle dog."

The modern doctrine of "work-life balance" dictates that you shouldn't take your work home with you. But if you want to know what sustains veterinarians through the profession's downsides—years of training, high debt, relatively low pay, frequent euthanasia—just look at the work they bring home.

Dr. Njeri Cruse, a dreadlocked, Brooklyn-born vet-for-hire who spends most days spaying and neutering pets for the ASPCA, lives with five cats, a mouse, and a ball python, all rescued from illness or neglect. Inbal Lavotshkin, the medical director of a New York–area emergency hospital, owns one dog abandoned by a family after it was hit by a car and another who was dying of heart failure—before Lavotshkin decided to pamper him for one last weekend and then, unwilling to let him go, wrangled him a pacemaker that saved his life.

Veterinarians are as varied as the animals they rescue (and sometimes adopt). They treat an astonishing array of creatures and biological systems, and just as there's no "typical" animal, there is no typical animal doctor. Maybe there was in the early 1940s, when the country vet James Alfred Wight (pen name James Herriot, author of *All Creatures Great and Small*) birthed his first calf. And even today, you can make some generalizations about a profession that, for all its range, requires a degree from one of only thirty American graduate schools and another couple dozen foreign institutions.

Our fictional "typical" veterinarian is, increasingly, female. She graduates with the same debt as a human doctor, well into the six figures and sometimes in excess of $300,000, but a much lower starting salary—a median of $70,000. She grew up around animals, whether on a family dairy or in a city teeming with strays of many species. In elementary school, college, or even well into another career, she became driven, possibly obsessed, with doing the very hard work it takes to earn a DVM or a VMD.

She may have been naturally introverted, favoring the innocence of animals to the social needs of humans, only to realize that it's impossible to be a good vet without liking people. She's euthanized countless animals in front of their owners, 80 percent of whom consider them family members, after coaching those owners through a level of cost-benefit analysis human patients rarely face. She is probably more susceptible to burnout and depression than most human doctors—but also open to the satisfaction of having heroically spoken up for creatures who can't describe their pain, and who ask for nothing in return for their companionship or their milk or the biodiversity that enriches our planet.

But no, there is really no typical veterinarian among the more than 100,000 who practice in the United States today, and nothing like a typical veterinary career. Michael Lund grew up in a North Dakota town of 1,300, thinking he might be a rancher or an architect before winding up at the ASPCA in New York, ministering to the pets of the urban poor. Elisha Frye is the daughter of a mixed-animal vet; she studied dance in Manhattan before following in her father's footsteps. M. Idina O'Brien was a world-class clarinetist until a car accident forced her into a second career— as an emergency-room veterinary surgeon. And Chick Weisse was earning his master's degree in economics when he took a night job in an animal hospital; a decade later he began inventing surgeries that changed the course of animal medicine.

Just as important as the idea that a vet can come from anywhere is the notion that one can go anywhere. The field is more complicated, in mostly good ways, than it ever was. It's harder to afford than it was even ten years ago, and it takes more skill and grit and flexibility, but it's also advancing further into procedures once reserved for humans; more responsive to pets and people in need; more humane to both animals and the overworked doctors who treat them; and more sensitive to the interconnectedness of all species. It's never been harder to be a vet, and never more exciting.

1

MONEY ISN'T IT: STARTING OUT

Michael Lund was raised in North Dakota, and though he moved to Brooklyn years ago, he has not shed the Lutheran sincerity of the Great Plains. A soulful do-gooder, he talks easily to strangers—he knew every single classmate in vet school—but he doesn't go in for the small talk of the typical extrovert. He makes intense, empathetic eye contact and shares oddly formal introspections ("It was pretty evident that it was not my dream anymore") with a downcast glare that almost makes you tear up. His blond hair flips down in a vaguely emo style, and his slight frame makes it easy to forget that he's six feet four inches tall.

Lund grew up in Crosby, North Dakota, ten miles from the Canadian border. He comes from an extended family of farmers and ranchers, and spent much of his youth among them. An hour's drive from the nearest veterinarian, Lund was the neighborhood's designated dog and cat sitter. "If someone was going out of town: 'Oh, call the Lund kid. He'll come by and take care of it.'" He arrived at Montana

State University without a specific major, favoring English and architecture but taking plenty of science courses, too. Halfway through school he met a vet one town over in Belgrade, Montana, who'd been practicing for years as an itinerant ranch veterinarian but had recently expanded from his garage to a mixed-animal practice. Lund wound up pulling shifts there.

For would-be vets like the young Lund, working as a vet assistant or tech is both a prerequisite and a gateway drug. The job can be a career of its own, akin to nursing, but for teenagers or college students interested in a veterinary career it's an essential stepping stone. In contrast to human medicine, vets techs and assistants don't have to be licensed, and for the medically curious, it's much easier to get your hands dirty at a vet clinic than a human practice. At least a little bit of such prior experience is virtually required for admission to vet school.

"With human medicine, you can't touch the people," says Olivia Love, a recent graduate of Colorado State's DVM program. Growing up in New Mexico, she would ride out on farm calls with animal doctors, and during college she spent summer breaks helping out. She was torn between human and animal medicine in college, but veterinary care gave her the opportunity to work hands-on before submitting a single application. Soon she was hooked.

For those who grew up maybe a little too attached to

pets, early tech jobs offer a chance to develop a professional distance from their emotions. Johanna Ecke, an associate in a New Orleans clinic, was a sensitive child; *Bambi* left her sobbing. While she took a pre-vet track at Tulane, "I wasn't certain I could handle the emotional aspect," she says. Even her parents wondered if she was up for it. But after Hurricane Katrina, she became an assistant at the Magazine Street Animal Clinic. "I got a lot of exposure to the realistic side"—and the confidence it took to apply to vet school. After graduating, she came back to Magazine Street. In a competitive field, many vets return to the practices where they had their first jobs and their earliest mentors.

The flip side of all that opportunity is the uncomfortable fact that vet technicians make a median of $32,000 a year. The class gap between career techs and veterinarians is wide and growing; in areas with high numbers of skilled immigrants, tech positions are filled with recent arrivals who were vets in their home countries, getting by on tech salaries while saving up for expensive vet licensing exams.

But getting into vet school takes more than experience; it takes an early awareness of the prerequisites you need (usually a premed track plus a few ecology or animal science courses). Premed students get plenty of advice, but would-be vets often have to look a little harder to find mentors. For Michael Lund at Montana State, it took persistence. "I kept trying to get a real conversation with my pre-vet advisor," he says, "but she was busy; she worked part-time. At some point, my mom marched in there and found this lady and reminded her that I should be given a chance."

Inbal Lavotshkin, now the medical director of VERE South, a Brooklyn emergency animal hospital, didn't get the advice she was looking for, so she looked elsewhere. At Rutgers University, she was a middling student well into her junior year, and doesn't necessarily regret it. "I think I grew as a person by not being completely straight-edge," she says. An ecology major, she visited Australia on a volunteer conservation trip and learned a lot about the biology of the animals. "I realized that my passion was in medicine," and that practicing it might be the way to "give back" to the planet.

Just before the start of her senior year, Lavotshkin walked into the office of Rutgers's vet-school advisor, who told her that it was too late to get all her prerequisites. She sought a second opinion from her ecology professor. On his advice, she wrote an essay explaining her transition and made a private commitment to get straight A's, which she did. She had to spend a summer catching up on chemistry and calculus. It wasn't that hard; it just took confidence and focus.

"I was a few steps behind," says Lavotshkin. "But we all end up in the same place. I would never tell someone in college that it's too late." For every vet who sailed straight through into vet school, there's one who spent one or two or four years after college in post-baccalaureate classes fulfilling her requirements, or in clinics doing the grunt work.

Few vets exemplify the never-too-lateness of the DVM track better than M. Idina O'Brien, an ER surgeon in suburban Virginia. Her childhood dream had nothing to do with animals. "My mom took me to see *The Nutcracker* when I was four years old," she says. "Every little girl was looking at the ballerinas, but I was fascinated by the women in the orchestra pit." So she requested a clarinet. O'Brien graduated from Juilliard and spent a decade performing with ensembles around the world. Then, in her early thirties, she was in a devastating car accident, which put her in the hospital for months. O'Brien had a life-threatening head injury and a severed nerve in her hand. "So that was the end of that career," she says, with the casual air of someone who thinks little of minor obstacles like a life-altering hospitalization. "I'd never imagined doing anything other than being a musician."

O'Brien's mother gave her six months to figure out a new career. One evening, over dinner, "I said, 'I want to apply to vet school.' No one said anything for a couple minutes, and I was like, 'Okay, what's going on?' Finally my mother said, 'You don't even have a high school education.' Well, you never tell me I can't do anything." To anyone aspiring to be a vet, she offers two hard-learned lessons: First, "There has to be something in your personality that gets to your goal no matter what." And second, "Find yourself a mentor."

O'Brien found hers while still recovering from her accident, thanks in part to her beloved dog. One day she summoned up the courage to tell her animal's vet, Dr. Louis Malacrida, about her plans. "He was probably a little skeptical himself," O'Brien says, but he invited her to work for him. The first day she showed up in a silk dress and was sent home to change. She volunteered until Dr. Malacrida insisted on paying her, and soon he let her see clients on her own. In her vet-school yearbook she'd write: "Dr. Malacrida, I have you to blame for this, and I can't thank you enough."

Juilliard had a post-baccalaureate program through Columbia University, which she completed in three semesters. "It was a little challenging," says O'Brien, with her knack for understatement. Her first application to vet school was submitted on a Friday; a letter of rejection followed on Monday, leading her to wonder if they looked past the first page. But her post-bac advisor advocated for her. She persuaded O'Brien to move to Philadelphia and apply to the University of Pennsylvania, where she was eventually accepted as an in-state student.

Her mother remained protective and skeptical. "You're in a different world now," she told her daughter. "You're not twenty-five. What you did before is going to be held against you." She may have been wrong about her daughter's prospects, but she was right about this. Vet school began with a stint in the college hospital's emergency room. "The first thing I did was introduce myself, and a head nurse said to me, 'You're not a musician, are you?' Well I wasn't anymore, so I said no. She said, 'Oh good, because I heard we're spoon-feeding some Juilliard reject through vet school.'"

Years later, one teacher confessed that much of the faculty had opposed her acceptance. O'Brien now conducts about a dozen prospective-student interviews a year for Penn, and she tries to stand up for students with artistic backgrounds. "I think they're realizing the value of someone having a different lens. When something doesn't work out"—say, on an operating table—"you have to rely on your creativity." She believes her experience playing music in front of huge audiences gave her the confidence to perform in the emergency room. "In music if you make a mistake, you have to go forward." The same ethic applies in the ER.

O'Brien's concerns are echoed by the Association of American Veterinary Colleges (AAVMC), whose decade-long diversity drive is bearing fruit not just in racial and economic terms but also in the kinds of people admitted. "Many of our schools have adopted a more holistic admissions process that allows for criteria other than test scores," says AAVMC CEO Andrew Maccabe.

Today's programs admit not just former dance majors

but also lawyers, farmers, and even a few disenchanted doctors. The crucible of vet school tends to burn away the differences in experience—eventually. Students from all kinds of backgrounds have to adjust their expectations. Harvard honors graduates suddenly find themselves in the middle of the pack, competing with kids who were raised stitching up cows. Those with years of vet-tech training bump up against straight-A overachievers. Frye, who majored in dance and biology at Marymount Manhattan College, says she "was not prepared for the level of intensity" at Cornell. "I failed the midterm and thought I was gonna flunk out. But then I was a C student, and then a B student."

And now, she's a vet: mission accomplished. Older students tend to enter vet school a little more focused on goals than grades. Early on at Penn, Dr. O'Brien published papers on immuno-parasitology. She expected to go into research before falling in love with patient care in her third year— and even then, she held herself to her own standards. "If there were sixty questions on a test and twenty were sheep questions, I'm not going to spend that much time learning about sheep," she says. "Because the chances of me touching them are zero. So even if I got an eighty on that test, I still got one-hundred percent."

Ken Osborn was a dairy farmer before going to vet school at the age of thirty-nine. He was bemused by all the young strivers around him at Cornell—in particular a twenty-one-year-old student named Becky. "Whiz kid, graduated early, sailed through college," says Osborn. She was in his study group for one class, which culminated in one all-important final exam. Their results were placed in their mailboxes. "I got my grade and I'm walking down the hall, so happy. And I run into Becky, and she looks like she's ready to cry. And I say 'What's wrong?'" It turned out they both got a B-plus. The difference was that Becky might never have earned less than an A before.

It's in the fourth year of school, when students get to work hands-on with sick animals, that skill levels begin to equalize. By then, in most schools, they have begun to track into broad categories—large-animal, wildlife, and especially small-animal. More than two-thirds of the members of the American Veterinary Medical Association (AVMA) report working exclusively with companion animals.

MICHAEL LUND HAD NO choice but to apply to a vet school out of state. North Dakota is one of twenty-one states with no vet schools. Lund still managed to pay in-state tuition at Colorado State University, thanks to one of many exchange programs whereby non-vet states compensate vet states, sometimes in return for a student's commitment to work in his home state for a while. But students in some of the most populous states, including New Jersey and Connecticut, can't apply as residents. The difference in tuition can add up to more than $100,000. For example, Colorado State charges $30,000 per year for in-state residents and $56,000 for out-of-state, meaning that Lund, who paid the lower fee, is *only* $60,000 in debt seven years later. Lavotshkin, who grew up in New Jersey, owes $330,000. Asked how she deals with it, she replies, "Denial."

The debt-to-income ratio is the single greatest challenge in veterinary practice today. Not long before the turn of the millennium it was 1-to-1—meaning the average debt equaled the average annual starting salary. Today it's over 2-to-1 and growing. That's because debt has doubled in the past fifteen years, to a 2015 median of $156,000, while starting incomes have risen only 15 percent. The AVMA's 2015 annual report charted a handy metric called "net present value." This is the difference between what you'd earn as a vet over a lifetime, after paying off your debt, versus what you'd make if you hadn't gone into vet medicine at all.

All other things being equal, women came out about $200,000 ahead. Men, who earn more across all fields, actually came out negative for the first time in 2014. (That said, they still start out earning slightly more than their female classmates.) Dr. Justine Lee, founder of the popular website VETgirl, worries it's becoming a "pink-collar profession," typecast as women's work and compensated accordingly.

Today, 80 percent of vet students are women, an astonishing turnaround since 1970, when 89 percent were men. The proportion of working vets who are women is 55 percent, and set to skyrocket as boomers retire.

What's behind the debt problem is under some dispute, but the 2008 recession hit the field particularly hard. The number of pets and vet visits declined, dragging inflation-adjusted salaries down with them, even as the cost of tuition went up. Pet ownership and spending has recovered since, but not much. Maccabe of the AAVMC pins the tuition increase on the decline in state funding, which has hit public graduate schools hardest. (Almost all veterinary schools are in public land-grant universities.)

But there is no shortage of aspiring vets, and schools have made up for decreased funding by accepting more of them. This actually made the debt problem worse, because most of the additional students pay higher out-of-state tuition. Add to that a flood of students from foreign schools, which the AVMA has accredited rapidly in recent years. There will be nearly nine hundred grads from foreign programs this year, fully qualified to practice. And many of those schools, especially Ross University, a very big for-profit school in the Caribbean, cost more to attend.

There may soon be too many vets. At the very least there is too great a supply of pet-care services relative to demand. "I would say most vets do not encourage people to go into vet medicine," says VETgirl's Dr. Lee. And as supportive as she is of the community, she isn't sure she'd advise young people to consider it today—"unless they're very rich," she says, half-joking. "If you're passionate about it, absolutely consider it. You just have to be cognizant about the debt and the work-life balance."

Vets may be awakening to the costs, but almost none of those I spoke with, regardless of age, specialty, or profession, would have made a different choice. (Whether they'd prefer a less crowded field of competitors is another question.) Very few of them personally regretted going into the field—not for all the debt, or the stress, or the long hours. Still, like Dr. Lee, they sounded a note of caution: go into the field with your eyes open. One vet surgeon, Jesse Terry, puts it this way. "I have a little son, and when he's older I'll tell him: 'There's a lot of fulfillment in this career, but you need to understand that you're not going to get rich. There are easier ways to make a living, so if you're going to do it you have to do it for the right reasons, and money isn't it.'"

A graduating vet may not have thought much about debt during school, but all that changes when the first bill arrives. It's against this backdrop that fewer than half of graduates go on to an internship—a year of rounds through various specialties—which is mandatory in human care but not in vet medicine. When I met Olivia Love, the intern who had chosen animal medicine over human because it was more hands-on, she was going through her emergency-room rotation—and visibly spent. She'd arrived at 6:30 a.m. and hoped to leave before 8:00 p.m., but a flood of emergencies that night would force her to stay until midnight. "I definitely have moments when I don't want to be doing this anymore, and I think it's a product of the internship."

Some vets told me they considered internships to be little more than a source of cheap labor. But Love wasn't the only one to tell me that she'd learned more in six exhausting months than in her last two years of vet school. For many students it's a way of crossing potential specialties off the list—learning, for instance, that internal medicine requires a lot of overtime, or that critical care is too intense for them. The latter was Love's conclusion. "Just general practice for me," she says. "I need some time to recover."

If you're even thinking of specializing, an internship is a must. Some specialties require two—a year rotating through departments and a year in the chosen specialty. No one who achieves success in a specialty finds those requirements too onerous a burden. As one successful surgeon put it to me, "Those couple of years were a blink of an eye in the scope of my career."

The career is what matters, of course. And the wonderful thing about vet medicine is that it's not a single career but a whole universe of them. Each one is a distinct ecosystem, with its own quirks, challenges, and exhilarating moments of joy.

2

CREATURES GREAT AND SMALL: ON THE FARM

Michael Lund decided against an internship. He thought only of heading back home—not exactly to the town where he grew up, but nearby, in the Badlands. Semi-arid big-sky plains stippled with scenic bluffs, this iconic American landscape represented "true cattle country" to Lund, a place of both solitude and close communities. Like a latter-day James Herriot, Lund wanted to travel between town and farm, enmeshed in the social fabric, treating creatures great and small. But rural life was changing, especially in North Dakota in the early years of the oil boom.

"Small-town farming and ranching was something I could understand," Lund explains. But he couldn't relate to the growing number of out-of-towners, there to make money at the expense of the land. "The oil boom typically forgets about the local people." He moved instead to Minot, a town of 40,000, but still found himself, incredibly, being priced out of a state he'd always considered a refuge. The cost of living was rising much faster than the pay for a rural vet. Lund realized that if he wanted to make ends meet, he might have to leave.

More generally, he was getting restless. The life of a mixed-animal vet is not for everyone. (A little over 10 percent of vets work on farm animals, depending on how you parse the numbers.) Those who practice it were either to the farmhouse born or lured away from urban lives by dreams of quiet, space, and the opportunity to be embedded in a community rather than a service industry. The lure has got to be powerful because, like most jobs in rural America, it often involves lower salaries, less stability, and a lot of driving. Also—there's no other way to put this—it stinks.

THE MOST POPULAR BUMPER sticker you'll see around Cornell University is ITHACA IS GORGES, a reference to the dramatic little canyons that cut through the region. The second most popular is TEN SQUARE MILES SURROUNDED BY REALITY, a reference to its being a liberal island in the midst of rolling dairy farms and gun shows. Driving northeast from campus, you know you've hit "reality" when the NPR affiliate statics out into scratchy country music and the manicured antique houses of Dryden give way to the strip malls and wheat fields of Cortland, New York. That's where Midstate Veterinary Services is located, conveniently central to every dairy and horse farm this side of Syracuse.

"Last year we had an open winter," says Ken Osborn, the farmer-turned-vet who was so happy to earn his B-plus at Cornell. He's referring to the lack of snow, a notable contrast to what we're now skidding through in a four-by-four packed willy-nilly with all manner of cords, syringes, notepads, pliers, and medicine packs. It's Osborn's work truck, property of Midstate (which is also partly his property; he's one of its four partners). The wipers strain against a lake-effect snow squall, and the vehicle's mild, sweet reek portends the morning ahead.

Osborn has a drawl that sounds almost Midwestern, and he looks much more like a farmer (which he was in the first half of his life) than today's (mostly female, suburban) vets. Behind slender, round wire-framed glasses are eyes crinkled in a perpetual sunburnt squint. He wears faded overalls and galoshes over work boots (as do I), and he speaks with clipped country innocence about the impressive Christmas tree he saw in the town square of Homer, New York. "It's not Rockefeller Center but I kinda like it."

He studied animal science as an undergrad, took all the vet prerequisites, and just missed getting into vet school. Then and now, many students don't get in on the first try—about 40 percent do and another 10 percent get in later. Osborn was ambivalent about vet school anyway. So he wound up working as a herdsman and, eventually, owning a small beef farm of his own. Then a midlife divorce led him to a fork in the road. The vet who tended to his animals suggested he reapply to veterinary school, and he did. He graduated from Cornell in 2001, the year his son Kasey entered the same program.

Osborn's roots in farming aren't typical of even a farm vet, but they help him navigate crucial relationships. The farm vet is the farmer's collaborator—an advocate for animal and herd health to be sure, but also a partner in maximizing the creature's productivity.

This morning, we're headed to New Hope View Farm, where Sarah Cough, herd manager and the owner's daughter, will accompany Osborn on a "preg check." The doctor will palpate roughly sixty-five of the farm's thousand milk cows to determine whether they're pregnant; check in on an ailing specimen or two; and inseminate three cows with frozen embryos retrieved from another, genetically more desirable cow. This last procedure is the real reason Osborn is here. Artificial insemination involves "flushing" eggs from a super-ovulated cow of high-end genetic stock and implanting them into surrogate cows on workaday milk farms like this one. Not every vet is trained in this modern art; Osborn is really a specialist in farmer's clothing.

Today's country vet practice bears little resemblance to that of the folksy Yorkshire doctor popularized in James

Herriot's *All Creatures Great and Small*, and it isn't just the frozen embryos and ultrasounds and automatic milking machines. For one thing, Osborn's ten-doctor practice gives vets most of their nights off. "The old James Herriot model where you had the neighborhood vet and he was on call all the time, that isn't mainstream anymore," he says—not when clinics like his have to compete for graduates with more professionalized and flexible suburban practices. There's still plenty of driving, and emergencies might not be tended to for an hour; as a result, more farmhands are learning how to check for pregnancies and perform basic procedures. But they'll never replace vets, who are licensed to administer drugs—and they certainly can't implant an embryo.

Twenty minutes into the drive, we pull off I-81 in the direction of a misty hill and slowly approach the farm. To our left, a series of massive barns emit a chorus of moos; to our right is a tent city of calves, each milling about a hut sheltered from the snow. "Good morning!" Osborn says to Sarah Cough. "She's a Cornellian, of course," he tells me. Cough studied animal nutrition before returning to work for her father when he expanded from a hundred cow farm to this operation.

The facilities are impressively automated, from the mechanical milkers to temperature-activated shades and V-shaped scraping machines that sluice waste toward the

walls every couple minutes. Headlocks are set to stay open
unless activated on the occasion of, say, a vet putting his
arm deep into the cow's rectum to feel for a vesicle on the
fallopian tube (a sign of pregnancy). Before the pregnancy
checks, Osborn takes a quick look at a young heifer with a
dislocated shoulder.

"They got to horsin' around and she ran into something,"
says Cough, in an accent halfway between Pennsylvania and
Fargo. "Occasionally the young ones get better," says Osborn. "But you can't pop it back in like they do in humans."
The problem is that you can't tell a cow to stay off the leg.
Time and rest is the best prescription—but a tricky one for
an animal born to move and not given to instruction. "We'll
occasionally open them up surgically," Osborn offers. "No
thanks," says Cough, who knows the cost-benefit analysis.
"I love her, but I don't love her that much." If the heifer
doesn't heal she'll be sent off for slaughter. This is no great
tragedy, just the way of life on the farm.

And with a quick pivot, we head deeper into the barn,
splashing through an ankle-deep mire of manure and urine.
Osborn compliments Cough on her purple Crocs, which
are looking less purple by the second. They're a Christmas
gift from her husband. "Not that I dislike brown but not everything needs to be brown," she says. Everything around
us is, except for the speckled Holsteins.

As we pass between rows of cows, posteriors always

pointed in our direction, the odor ranges from unpleasant to nauseating, at least to the uninitiated. "I can't stand the smell of cigarette smoke," Cough says while gossiping about a farm couple they know. I ask the obvious question. "Oh, I'd take cow shit any day," she says. "You're never gonna get lung cancer from cow manure," says Osborn. That is true, and there is a sweet tang to it. The urine is worse.

Like human doctors and nurses, vets have to develop a tolerance for blood and guts. In his early mixed-animal days in North Dakota, Michael Lund had a moment when it got the better of him. He was once tasked with removing a dead and decayed calf fetus from its mother (who survived). "I had to chop up and pull out bit by bit this decomposing calf," says Lund. "It was disgusting. I think I vomited a couple of times. The owner was laughing his head off because it wasn't his problem anymore. He's like, 'That's the best hundred dollars I've ever spent.'"

Osborn's dairy visit is a little less dramatic. He rolls a three-foot-long latex glove over his left arm all the way to the shoulder and clips it to a sling that covers half his chest. Farm vets often use their nondominant arm, the theory being that they can still write with the other one in the rare event that, say, a spooked cow makes a sudden move and wrenches the doctor's submerged arm. After many years of preg checks the arm sometimes rises up of its own accord, as if stuck in an invisible shoulder cast. Osborn has never been seriously injured, but Cough's father recently had shoulder surgery.

The next hour follows a semiregular beat, interrupted by the occasional ornery cow slipping out of her lock. "Thirty-six days," Cough says, announcing the time elapsed since a cow's last insemination. "Pregnant," Osborn says, marking a green line on its flank, or "Open" if it didn't take, with a green circle, so it can be bred again immediately. (More calves mean more lactation and more milk.) These days many vets prefer to use an ultrasound machine, which attaches to their fingers so they can see the embryo on a handheld screen. It's more accurate and shows pregnancies a few days earlier, so hyper-efficient dairies prefer it. But it takes more time and money, and palpation works just as well. Any reasonably skilled doctor, or even a farmhand, can declare a pregnancy by simply inserting an arm into the rectum and feeling through the lining of the colon for a little bump on the nearby fallopian tube.

The most notable change in farm care has more to do with theory than technology. More vets and farmers alike are paying attention to herd health, which encourages both productivity and prevention. C-sections used to be very common—at least one a month when Osborn was starting out. "Now it's once a year." ("Pregnant!" he says, interrupting himself.) Dairies pay more attention to factors like housing, management, and genetics, resulting in less disease and easier pregnancies. "Sick cows are expensive—and heartbreaking," says Cough.

New Hope View is one of the better-managed farms in the area, per Midstate's owners. Vets are in a service profession, and not given to scolding their clients—who are generally receptive to advice in any case. Only once has a client's management gotten so bad—"hygiene and just slovenliness," recalls Osborn—that Midstate dropped the farm for treating its animals poorly.

"Pregnant!" Osborn says again, shaking off glops of manure. "That one was a Swiss embryo," Cough says with a note of pride. One day she hopes to have a pen full of Brown Swiss cows—a breed that makes richer milk and has a lovely tan coat. A grown one passes between us, sporting a red pompadour. "I have a little fetish for Brown Swiss," she says. That's the kind of frozen embryo we're waiting for, from a farm that specializes in breeding. Cough will birth any resulting calves and return them to the mother cow's farm, but sometimes she arranges to keep some. Unlike most of the Holsteins (save for a few "pets"), all her Brown Swisses have names (Granola, Sweet Pea, Gizmo, Swissy). Later, she'll take us out to a separate shed of Brown Swiss calves; cooing and petting them, Cough the bean-counting herd manager will turn into an everyday pet owner in love. Back here in the big, smelly pens, the numbered cows get a little bit less doting, but just as much respect. Both farmer and vet have genuine affection for their animals—partners in a life cycle of human sustenance.

At last, the frozen Swiss embryos arrive. Carrying them in a small tank steaming with liquid nitrogen is Mike Reinhardt, from a farm down the road. Inside are twenty-six eggs, which a "flush" vet has extracted—using saline solution—from the uterus of a super-ovulated prize-winning Brown Swiss. In the back office, Reinhardt pulls out three plastic straws, one by one. Osborn thaws these "embryo transfer guns" in a bath of eighty-five-degree water, lays them out on a towel, and covers them with blue plastic sheaths. "Then I put it inside my shirt," he says, for the walk down to the recipients. The temperature under his arm is about eighty-five—something Osborn learned by driving between farms with a thermometer tucked in his armpit. "We ought to have something more sophisticated," he jokes. This isn't true IVF; the embryos aren't fertilized outside the cow's body. The techology exists—there is a large national IVF chain that offers sex-selective semen and cloning—but you'd need a facility close by.

Osborn paces at double speed with three valuable tubes in his shirt. Waiting for him are three big animals, each eight days past her heat, with tight, spiraling cervixes that require a trained hand to push the tubes through. Osborn has no trouble with the first two but takes a full five minutes on the third. "They do test your patience sometimes," he says. His left arm is shoulder-deep in the rectum, feeling the cervix through the membrane to help guide the sheathed gun, which his right hand pushes into the vagina. Another cow makes an ill-timed advance on us, and Cough urges me to give her a shove before she knocks the tubes out of Osborn's shirt. "Just hit her, she won't feel it. Poke her in the ribs!" Finally she just does it herself. The cow slightly alters her trajectory, like an asteroid successfully diverted.

"Well, this is a tough one," Osborn says before finally finding purchase and pressing the gun's plunger. A month from now, he'll be palpating the same cow, this time to see if a new Brown Swiss is on its way—maybe another velvety pet for New Hope View Farm.

After a final set of preg checks we head back to the Cortland office, which is really a purpose-built oversize shed. The back half of Midstate is unfinished, warehouse-like, stocked with medicines of all shapes and sizes. Depositing our overalls straight into the washer (something is always being laundered at a vet clinic), we head past a large operating room, through a set of small-animal exam rooms, and up to the front, a spacious and completely ordinary waiting room. Even with the faint musk of dog fur and antiseptic, it smells great.

Elisha Frye strides in through Midstate's back door, wearing a green fleece hat, a broad smile, and overalls and galoshes that she won't be taking off any time soon.

"Hi Ken! This is my kitty," she says, speaking twice as fast as Osborn and holding up a carrier. Inside is one-eyed Mr. Winks, a large, fluffy orange tabby. At home, he's Sandy's feline counterpart and fellow rescue animal. Frye didn't personally save his life, as she did Sandy's, but now she might have to. "He has a fever of 104," she says to Osborn. "He went down but then he spiked again this morning. I wonder if he just got stressed and maybe cold."

"I don't know anything—I'd treat him the same as beef cattle," Osborn jokes. The mutual incomprehension of large- and small-animal vets is a reliable source of humor at a practice like this—big enough for a complete division of labor. Frye is one of two doctors here, out of ten, who treat all sizes.

Frye walks over to a desk and talks a tech into giving Mr. Winks an IV and some fluids for what was determined yesterday, after a round of X-rays and bloodwork, to be a "fever of unknown origin." ("Put him outside, that'll cool him down!" suggests another cow vet.)

Frye attends to small animals only once a week (aside from her own two pets). She's just come in from a preg check at a dairy half the size of Sarah Cough's, and she has to be back there shortly. They had a case with a displaced abomasum; occasionally, in a cow that's recently given birth, one digestive chamber (aka the "true stomach") will float out of place in her body cavity, requiring urgent but routine surgery. The whole thing is done while the cow is awake and standing. "Once in a great while they lay down," Frye says—which can lead to a fatal infection of the incision. That hasn't happened to her in a long time.

Frye could have just stayed out at the dairy—it's a half hour drive each way in the bad weather—but she needed to come back and see to Mr. Winks. And with a five-month-old daughter at home, she also needed to pump milk, and wasn't inclined to do so in the barn.

Vet clinics of all kinds have become more responsive to family needs; they'd better be, now that the job is becoming overwhelmingly female. (Frye is one of three new mothers in the ten-vet practice.) But that doesn't mean it's smooth sailing: there are struggles in farm medicine, physical and otherwise, that many of her colleagues would rather not deal with. "It's really hard being a mom and doing the job, especially on call," she says later. Like many large-animal vets who become mothers, she's considering switching to pets only. The unpredictable hours, manual labor, and time lost to long drives and house calls can make farm medicine a tough fit for new mothers. "It's just a reality," says Frye.

Work-life balance is a common topic of any professional conversation, but especially in this field. Justine Lee wrote a long post on her VETgirl blog headlined, "Why You Should Stop Your Veterinary Career and Have Kids Now!" (She finally did, at forty-three.) Luckily, Frye's husband, Chris, is on an academic schedule and available to fill in. Today, school is out and Chris is home with the baby. But, as he'll tell me later, cradling the infant in his arms, "It doesn't seem like there's ever really a great time to have a kid when you're a veterinarian."

Frye walks over to the back wall of an office, a third of which is covered with a huge black-and-white map of the region. It looks like the wall of a car-service dispatch, and it's dotted with red numerals one through four, marking concentric circles of increasing distance from the clinic. Beside it is a laminated sheet listing the prices of an ambulatory call, ranging from $30 (a routine cattle call in Zone 1) to $200 (a horse emergency up by Seneca Falls, an hour away in perfect weather). That doesn't include animal care, just the drive out, but considering gas and the doctor's time, it's a steal.

Back out on the road, Frye gives me a taste of chocolate milk from the dairy we're headed to—a more easily digestible strain. It's delicious. The farm is now in the hands of the founder's homeschooled grandchildren, and it's a little more laissez-faire than New Hope View. "Sometimes there's animals that need to be put down that aren't," she says. "I think they're just a bit disorganized."

On a drive even snowier than Osborn's farm visit, Frye talks about how she got here. Her father is a mixed-animal vet who grew up in the suburbs but "didn't really like the crowded, congested life." He found the antidote on the out-skirts of Rochester, in far Western New York, "one of those counties that had more farms than people." Frye tried to rebel in turn, going to college in Manhattan. And yet, here she is. She specialized in equine medicine at Cornell, and still treats plenty of horses—a more graceful and prized species than cows, to be sure. But when I ask what a nice Jewish girl who went to school on the Upper East Side is doing on the business end of dozens of cows a day, she has an answer.

"I enjoy being around cows as a species, just very sweet and fearful. And I like ultrasounding"—seeing the preg-nancy for herself. "I don't think I'd like to be in an office all day." All things being equal, "I'm a little uptight when I'm doing small-animal. It can be much more formal. I'm on a first-name basis with the farmers and 'Doctor' with the small animals." Pet owners are "looking to you for all the answers," but on a farm, "if something goes wrong—I haven't killed that many things but it happens, and it's ex-tremely stressful for me—they're not going to blame me, because we have the relationship."

Early on, before she built up that trust, Frye wasn't al-ways so confident in her skills. One time, she inserted a tube into a horse's windpipe instead of its esophagus, which "essentially drowned the horse." In the heat of the moment, she overheard the owner say, "She fucking killed my horse."

But when she came back for the autopsy, "he was very forgiving"; he even called her boss to check in on her emotional state. Frye was distraught, but what she didn't realize was that she'd made a surprisingly common rookie error. (In fact, exactly the same mishap is cited on page nine of *All Creatures Great and Small*.) She wondered if she was really cut out for the work. Her husband told her, "You can either stop working with horses, or you can learn the procedure." She's come to accept that helping horses is worth the risk of losing them.

Still, it's more than just the love of animals that motivates farmers, and veterinarians, too. "You're feeding the world," says Frye. Her boss, Paul Coen, whom I catch later at the office, seconds that conviction. He grew up in Queens, the son of a book editor, but like Frye's father he wanted a rural life. He studied international relations in college, but graduated with the notion that NGO work was too bureaucratic and far-removed from the land. He wound up teaching agriculture in Sierra Leone. Intrigued by the role farming plays in economic development, he decided after graduation to work on a farm in Wisconsin. While earning another degree, this time in animal science, at the University of Massachusetts, he became good friends with a vet. "I'd never seen someone have so much fun in his work."

Now, he acknowledges, things have changed. "The role that a veterinarian has socially and economically, that really attracted me, naively in some ways," he says. But the "James Herriot view of the work" is no longer operative. "Farms have gotten very large, and more efficient. We've been in it a long time, we've seen farms grow and we've contributed to the growth, and there's a lot of exciting things going on from a technology and systems standpoint. It's a very different kind of thing that has to motivate you now."

Systems are motivation enough for Coen's co-owner, Dave Brandstadt, a jockish man with straw-colored hair in a baseball cap bearing the logo of Zoetis, the world's largest animal drug manufacturer. He and Coen merged smaller businesses to create Midstate ten years ago, after realizing their territory overlapped (farm vets are a little like gangs that way, each with his own turf). "I'm much better at the economic side of things than the emotional side," says Brandstadt, who thinks of himself as a kind of medical consultant, ferreting out "underperforming" areas on his clients' farms.

Frye, on the other hand, still gets her kicks by getting into a truck and driving miles to fix up a cow. The closer we get to that disorganized family farm in her SUV, the thicker the snow gets, and the narrower the winding roads. It's a beautiful, treacherous drive. By the time we get to the dairy we can barely see outside the car, and the only visible driveway is so steep we need to creep down at a mile per hour. Through the whiteout you can just make out a low-slung barn in the valley. "I'm gonna try not to die on this road here," Frye says, feeling apprehensive but adventurous. She pushes a "snow" button on the dash, and nothing changes. "You should have come in the spring," she says. It's the other three seasons that she lives for, when squalls give way to pleasant breezes and the landscape reminds her of why she chose this life over small-animal suburbia.

"*Hola, cómo estás,*" Frye says to a farmhand, after we've safely descended. "*Los vacas con la leche especial, si?*" She wants to see where the fancy digestible milk is stored. Frye recently applied for (and didn't get) a grant from the American Association of Bovine Practitioners to learn two things—embryo implantation and Spanish. Many of the farmhands are seasonal Latino migrants. Seth, one of the grandsons on the farm, meets us and leads us to the sick cow. We pass through a dark, muddy, and very noisy room. This is where Seth thought Frye might want to operate.

"We can't do it here," says Frye. "It's too dark!"

"Outside?" Seth asks nonchalantly.

"Yeah, I think it should be all right, it's like, what, twenty-eight out?"

Just outside the room, the sick brown Jersey stands apart on a bed of straw under a sloping roof held up by posts. Frye overturns a blue plastic barrel and lays out her tools—clamps, scissors, catgut sutures. Ten feet away, a tractor moves to and fro, grinding and beeping. Snow blows in on unpredictable gusts. "Oh dear, this is not sterile, having snow on my surgery pack," says Frye. "But we're gonna roll with it. We don't really have a choice."

"She's not feeling really well," says Seth, patting the cow. Frye opts for a lower dose of sedative. Too much and she might lie down. Frye chats with Seth about their kids while shaving the animal's massive, slightly concave flank. The errant stomach chamber, having filled up with gas, is displaced to the left. You can hear it with a stethoscope—like the faint sound of a basketball hitting pavement.

"It's like a pin dropping—*tink!*" Frye says. While she talks me through the mechanics, a farm employee observes behind us. He takes a cell phone call at one point to discuss the acquisition of a missing tractor part. "Driveshaft's all in . . . It's the housing for that cylinder there . . ." Sometimes it's hard to tell the vehicle parts from the animal. It's all just intricate patch-ups and wonky machinery.

After administering a sedative under the tail and wiping down the shaved flank with alcohol, it's time to inject numbing Lidocaine. With a large needle Frye pokes holes in an arc over the surgical area, and the tough skin gives under pressure, like a thin piece of leather. To the cow this is little more than a finger prick, but blood still streams out from each puncture. Then Frye takes a large scalpel and cuts an eight-inch gash, through which her gloved hand soon follows.

"They're just so hardy," Frye says. "They don't need a surgical suite. I'm cutting into the right side, and hopefully if she lays down she'll go that way. Obviously it would contaminate everything if they laid down with this incision open." The cow sways slightly when Frye cuts through the peritoneal wall and sticks her arm in deeper, past her elbow, fishing around for the abomasum. A tractor comes deafeningly close.

Finding the stomach, Frye thrusts a sharp-ended tube called a trocar into the chamber, far beyond the incision. But no gas comes out, so she starts sucking on the other end of the tube to try and vacuum it out. "It's just not wanting to correct." Finally, she gets purchase on the chamber. She'll need to stitch it to the abdominal wall so it never displaces again, which means finding the pylorus, a nub at the end of the stomach.

The cow shifts. "Sorry, girl." The cow shifts more. "No, honey, hey, hey, hey." The cow leans into Frye . . . and lies down to the right. "Crap!" Frye takes her arm out and cups her hand over the wound, which is now just a few inches from the dirty straw.

"Come on, girl, hup, hup, hup!" she says. Seth brings a prod, like a little Taser, and starts stunning the cow with repeated shocks. "Seriously, this hasn't happened to me in like a year," Frye says during a pause. "This used to make me really anxious, but—" she seems quite anxious, actually, but not panicked. It's just one of those days at the office that keeps things interesting. "Hup, hup, come on, girl, hup." More beeps of the prod. Seth is now shocking the cow every two seconds; to the hulking cow, it might as well be a fly.

"Come on, girl," says Frye. "Hup, hup! Come on, hup, hup! Cow! You're making my life very difficult." Seth asks if she could finish the surgery this way; she says it might be impossible. She closes three clamps over the incision to minimize the exposure.

Clearly, we need more manpower. "Damn it," Frye says to Seth, "can you get somebody else to physically help you?" Another farmhand comes by. "Can you just shift her over that way?" She points toward the gate. He starts moving the cow . . . down toward Frye. "No, no, *por favor*!"

This goes on for another ten minutes. "You picked a good one to watch," Seth tells me. Finally, grudgingly, the cow gets up, nearly knocking over the barrel and its more or less sterile instruments. "Okay, cool, all right," says Frye. "Crisis somewhat averted. *Gracias*."

Frye offers a running post-non-mortem as she opens the cow back up, digs out the pylorus, and starts suturing with a thick, long scythe of a needle. "I gave her the low dose!" she says. "I think I was pulling on her guts and she was not feeling good. I should have read her as feeling sicker than they thought she was, I guess."

Fifteen minutes later, it's done. Frye prescribes two antibiotics. If the cow's incision had any contact with the straw, she may die of infection. As we trek through six inches of fresh snow back to the SUV, I ask if she's ever aborted a surgery. "That's the closest I've come to considering it," she says. "So you got to see the good and the bad, there you go. Well, that was just the ugly." To me it looked like what I'd read about the old days. James Herriot's first book opens with a physically exhausting, near-fatal procedure on a cow in the middle of a snowstorm. ("They didn't say anything about this in the books," he begins.) No amount of IVF or herd-management work can make farm medicine bloodless.

A few weeks later, I call in and get the news. The cow lived. Frye had succeeded, so far as it went. She began her career with a surgery she thought she'd botched—only to save a golden retriever's life and become her protector. Later, she made a few (inevitable) mistakes. But today she kept her cool under impossible conditions and saved a life in the process. For Frye, it'll be more than just a good story to tell. Cows aren't pets, but the job of healing them—of getting it right every time—can feel as important as saving a dog. Just as there's almost nothing more stressful than losing a patient, few moments are as exhilarating as keeping one alive. Being a vet means experiencing both.

3

THERE'S PEOPLE EVERYWHERE: SMALL-ANIMAL PRACTICE

If the country farm doctor represents the antiquated idyll of veterinary life, the mom-and-pop private practice is the modern paradigm—the vision of owning a storefront clinic where pets, clients, and colleagues feel like family. Though that dream, too, is increasingly elusive in the age of chain vets and big debts, it's still attainable for fortunate entrepreneurs like Dr. Catherine Wood. As a day at her new practice makes perfectly clear, the trick is not to get burned out or go broke before the business gets off the ground.

I visited Dr. Wood's Brooklyn clinic in early 2017, less than a year after she cofounded it. The waiting room stocks a collection of James Herriot stories—apropos for a place called All Creatures Veterinary Hospital. Wood is a friend of Michael Lund's, but nothing like him. Her personality— a mix of crisp sweetness and scathing wit reminiscent of Mary Poppins—is a little more in tune with the typical vet, who tends to score as an ISTJ on the Myers-Briggs personality test (the type some call "the logistician").

Though she was raised in England, Wood was born in Ithaca, New York, while her father was on sabbatical there. (He went on to design semiconductors for the Navy.) She has an accent that's roughly one-third English, one-third American, and one-third sibilant Baby Voice she adopts when speaking to or about the pets she treats. She feels that her passion for animals is hereditary. Her mother, who grew up on a dairy farm, always wanted to be a vet but couldn't make the grades. "So her main purpose for having children, she said, was to make the world a better place for animals."

Consequently, the Wood family's garage sheltered bunnies, hedgehogs, squirrels, and seagulls in various stages of repair. At age four, Wood wanted to be a ballerina; two years later she wanted to be a vet. The family returned to Ithaca when she was eight, starting her glide path through Cornell—undergrad followed by vet school, to which she earned a full scholarship. "I didn't tell too many people that because I think they'd kill me," she says.

Lawyers might dream of working at the ACLU, only to find themselves paying down debt by joining corporate firms; so it goes with vets. Many of them take wildlife courses and do externships at zoos or abroad, but very few of those can support themselves on it. Without any debt, Wood was able to not only save up for the clinic but also indulge a passion for wildlife medicine (which she also hopes to subsidize through private practice). Within two years of earning her DVM, she was working in Malawi on primates and in Cambodia on trafficked birds. But like Lund in the Badlands, she found that it takes more than a low cost of living to sustain a vet; it takes a market for pet care.

"That's part of the reason I started the clinic," she says. "Eventually I'm hoping to have the resources to do more creative things." She and her clinic partner, Erica Morgan, were working at another Brooklyn practice, but after a couple years they found the management to be "just too lackadaisical. Captainless ship." Together with another colleague, who is now their practice manager, they began a "three-year process of battling New York City real estate and bureaucracy" to start All Creatures.

First they had to find the right location. On morning jogs, Wood counted dogs per mile, and this busy corner of Crown Heights tallied up well. "I liked the mix of gentrification and also people that lived here for years and maybe never even got [their pet] a rabies vaccine." Despite some trouble with contractors, it was relatively easy to secure loans, since vet clinics are considered low-risk in comparison to enterprises such as restaurants.

Like a lot of businesses, though, they don't break even for a while. Wood makes her money, like many vets, from shift work. Every once in a while she does spays and neuters on a mobile ASPCA truck, but more frequently she spends a day or two a week pulling shifts in an emergency room, which pays $100 an hour.

Wood and Morgan haven't quite figured out the division of labor. "We have very different styles," says Wood. "I want everything laid out that we're going to do next month this month, and who's doing what, and what are the deadlines? And she's like, 'Oh, we'll just do it organically.' That's been the biggest stress."

Wood is aware of the knock on vets as doctors who don't want to deal with people. "But you end up dealing with an awful lot of people in vet medicine," she says. This is true on farms, in cities, and even in the African bush. "I hear, 'Oh, wildlife must be great—no clients!' No. You have to deal with charities and donors and wildlife rehabbers. There's people everywhere."

"First thing in the morning—I hate that," says Samantha, the All Creatures receptionist. "Contact us at twelve when we're caffeinated!" Samantha, Dr. Wood, and her two vet techs had barely gotten through the door on what was supposed to be a slow day, the Friday before Christmas, when they were chewed out by the owner of a pit bull mix for what she insisted was a botched spay surgery the day before. Never mind that the owner, a very worried-looking middle-aged woman, hadn't followed instructions; instead of waiting twenty-four hours to remove poor Millie's surgical cone, she took it off the minute they got home.

Wood tries to smooth things over in the waiting room, a cheery space in a jumble of clashing styles—bright blue paint behind the reception desk, half a cinderblock wall, Southwestern potted cactus and aloe plants, and a banner hung IN LOVING MEMORY of departed pets. "I'll probably do the repair sometime late this morning," Wood tells the owner. "Oh man, I'm sorry," the owner says, suddenly conciliatory. "Is she crazy back there?"

"She's happy!" says Wood. "She's a real happy dog."

Actually, Millie looks a little forlorn. She's down in the basement, a spare and clean space with three stacked rows of cages, one table for dental procedures, and—her next destination—a glassed-off room for more serious surgeries. Millie's in no evident pain right now, despite trailing raw, bright pink globs of fat from the open abdominal wound where she was spayed yesterday. Matty, a fit thirteen-year-old pit bull, whines two cages away, as if he knows that his simple cyst removal has to be postponed due to his neighbor's more pressing mishap.

Millie's spay patch-up is free of charge; that, along with Wood's British politeness, has appeased the owner for now. After she leaves, Wood clomps downstairs in exasperation. "I cannot stand when people are rude to staff and nice to me," she says. "I don't know how to deal with people like that except keep them at arm's length. She's worried about her dog, I get it. But *oh my God*, don't take the e-collar off after surgery!" She grunts. I ask if she's ever lost patience with an owner. "Probably not by most people's standards," she says.

By 9:30 a.m., Wood has already attended to a shepherd mix with diarrhea in an upstairs waiting room, and now there's Mr. Bun-Bun, an eight-year-old rabbit with a "head tilt" (dizziness probably caused by a protozoan in the inner ear). It's not even a surgery day—those are Wednesdays and Thursdays—but now she has to squeeze in two between patient appointments. "It stresses me out," she says. Then she gives Millie a slightly guilty look—"Oh, Millie," she sighs—as if to refocus on what matters, which is the animal's safe recovery.

Preparing for Mr. Bun-Bun's procedure, she puzzles out some medication orders on a computer in the basement office, trying to find the right codes for rabbits. Then she takes blood. "He's such a good Bun-Bun," she says, pouting her lips in her signature Baby Voice. They'll need to confirm the rabbit's ailment, but in the meantime she prescribes an antibiotic. The bill will come out to $350—a fraction of a human medical bill, but something that takes getting used to without the fig leaf of insurance. The owner puts the payment on two cards.

Next, Wood walks over to Matty and examines the cyst on his paw. "Now what are we gonna sedate you with?" Matty pants and whines. Sam the receptionist comes down the stairs. She has a habit of dropping in unannounced, as the clinic has no intercom. She asks for the okay to order a prescription. "Oh, and Olive. The ear is really bad," says Sam.

Right, her appointment with Olive. Wood pauses and breathes. "Moment of Zen," she says. "This client talks. Though she's really nice." We head into one of three exam rooms. Olive is a beautiful tan and white little pit bull. "Her ear's the worst," says the owner, "but under her tail is getting bad and then she's got this one hot spot under her belly here."

Olive is a repeat customer, "a loveable lemon." Wood already has her on an anti-inflammatory and a hypoallergenic diet. She asks when Olive was last in. "The days run together," she says apologetically. It's been three weeks, so she recommends a few more weeks on the diet. "If it comes back it's environmental, and she's probably gonna need medication for life." She turns to Olive in the Baby Voice—"Because you can't control New York City!" She and the owner proceed to baby talk in tandem. "Can't deal with New York!" "No, it'sh too much!" "And now you've got belly rubs," says Wood, following through on her threat with tickles and squeaks. Olive whistles along. "She's singing to us," says Wood. "She's wonderful." Maybe this is her moment of Zen. A few minutes later, the doctor heads back down to the basement to update her two techs on Millie's surgery. But before they can get started, she has another appointment.

Chompsky is a skinny little mutt with an atrophied eye. His owners, a young tattooed couple, adopted him a few days ago from a rescue group that brought him in from Korea, where he was probably bred for his meat (though he'd hardly make a decent meal). After a quick exam, Wood says the eye is probably congenital. "You're perfect," she Baby-Voices at Chompsky. "Making friends with every-body!" He's a little rough around the claws, so she orders an "emergency pedicure."

Efficiently cradling a shivering Chompsky, Wood walks down to the basement and hands him over to Lauren, one of her technicians. "He was gonna be a stew!" says Lauren. "But now you're a pet. Silver lining." The mutt yelps during his grooming, unused to the attention. "No blood, no blood," says Wood, asking his indulgence. Sam makes one of her too-frequent visits to tell of an owner who wants to bring in a cat with heart failure and a mass on its leg—but "refuses to give him anything but holistic medication." Wood suggests a clinic on Long Island.

"So guys, whatever happened to that chicken?" Sam asks suddenly. "Dead," says Jena, the other tech. "It was a broiler—it just couldn't stand up." Stray poultry-shop fugitives are more common in the city than you'd think; Lauren dealt with them constantly in a previous gig with the Wild Bird Fund in Manhattan. Wood handles exotic pets, too, but finds reptiles to be hard. Birds, at least, have "great veins."

Wood announces, out of the blue, "I'm ready for Christmas now, just ready not to be here. Actually, never mind. I'll be in the ER on Christmas," with a cat. This won't be her usual per diem work, but family time; she'll be down in Maryland catering to her mother's kitty's broken leg. "My mom's the worst client," Wood jokes about the woman who informed her she was born to heal animals. "She's terrible."

A few minutes later, Millie is sprawled spread-eagle in the glassed-in surgery suite, an anesthesia tube leading into her trachea. "Good heartbeat," Jena reports. Without ceremony, Wood snips the fat dangling from Millie's wound before slightly widening it. She nudges aside some internal organs. "There was some source of bleeding," she says a few minutes later. "I'm still not sure what it was. To explore it I'd have to make a bigger incision, but given this dog's history, we're not making it any bigger."

Jena asks how much longer it'll be; Millie's heart rate is dropping. "More fricking stitches," Wood says, explaining the delay. "All three layers were chewed through." She actually looks a bit relieved. The rupture has nothing to do with her technique. After her owner took off the e-collar, Millie tore apart the stiches binding the skin, the subcutaneous layer, and the abdominal body wall. "We usually do a single continuous layer of stitches," Wood explains, "but she chewed it out, so now she gets a lot, because I don't trust her—or the people."

As if on cue, Sam tromps down the stairs from reception. "Dr. Wood, were you aware that Junior is coming in for a recheck?"

Wood growls. "They were supposed to make an appointment."

"Yeah, the boyfriend just kind of walked in."

"Ear infection," says Wood. "I'll be there as soon as I can."

Back to Millie's stitch-up. "Just one more layer," she says, threading the skin. "Three layers. Skin glue, too. Goddamnit, I'd do Kevlar on this dog if I could." After thinking for a moment, she asks for a surgical stapler and staples down the length of the incision.

"Damn, Millie," Jena laughs. "She said, 'Not this time!'"

Wood nods slightly. "Never want to see you again. All right, that was beautiful." She looks up. Millie sports a fresh column of horizontal staples, the scars of a pit bull Frankenstein. "She looked pretty yesterday," Wood says loudly, then turns to Lauren and smirks. "If you could put an e-collar on, that would be great."

————

DR. WOOD IS NOT the only vet in the world who finds dealing with people harder than dealing with animals. It's intrinsic to the job, especially in private practice, that the vet, owner, and pet exist in an unstable love triangle: the pet's at the top, ideally receiving unconditional love from one human and unrestricted health care from the other, while the two humans in charge must navigate a professional relationship defined by wary trust and the exchange of money. In the absence of insurance—which roughly 3 percent of pet owners have in a country where even human health care is hard to afford—money inevitably leads to guilt. Vets feel guilty if forced to offer either too much care or too little; owners feel guilty if they spend too much money or too little.

As a result, vets say owners have become more demanding, more prone to both Googling and price shopping than they once were. Things seem particularly bad in the cities and suburbs of the Northeast. But the relationship is always fraught. People take their pets very seriously, and vets are an easy target for their stress. Forget torn-out stitches: doctors have been physically attacked, accused of murder, hounded in one case to suicide. "You're seeing clients on their worst day," says Jesse Terry, a vet surgeon. "As much as you might love your job, the reality is that no one wants to drop a few thousand dollars on their dog's knee or hear that their pet only has a few years to live."

Love them or hate them, any vet must learn to become a people person. "Client communication is something I've focused on a lot because it's a weakness of mine," says one vet at a suburban practice. "I'm always going to be an advocate for the animal," she says. It's difficult sometimes to paper over a conflict between the animal's needs and the owner's ideas, but recognizing the latter's perspective is also part of the job. This vet remembers a cat being brought in with a slow wasting disease; the owner was furious at being made to wait on what she saw as a critical case. "I said, 'You waited ten years to see a vet, and now you can't wait twenty minutes?'" She immediately regretted her own lapse in diplomacy, promising herself she'd do better.

Inbal Lavotshkin, the ER medical director in Brooklyn, has dealt with clients ranging from overzealous to abusive. On the day I visit her hospital, VERG-South, she is overseeing euthanasia on a beautiful retriever. The owners were at work while the ailing dog—who'd spent the night in intensive care—rapidly declined. By phone, they insisted on CPR, which has a rate of recovery below 5 percent. Twenty painful minutes after being revived, the dog is rasping his last breath. The owners were too distraught to make it to this final procedure; a resident injects the fatal barbiturate and gently strokes his head while Lavotshkin looks on, dab-

bing her eyes. A dilemma like this—being forced to pro-
long a dog's suffering, while the owner isn't even there—is
"something you don't think about very much when you're in
school. We think of them as family but legally speaking, the
animal is [the client's] property."

She tells a story from the other end of the spectrum—
abuse. A couple brought in a kitten with rib fractures and an
eye that was out of its socket. The boyfriend claimed he'd
been trying to give the kitty a bath and it slipped out of his
hands, but the story didn't match up with the injuries. All the
evidence pointed to violence, and Lavotshkin reported him to
the police. He was eventually arrested, and the cat was sent to
a foster home. "I hopefully helped a whole family situation,"
she says, by "opening the woman's eyes" to a pattern of domestic abuse. (Studies show a very strong correlation between
pet abuse and domestic violence.) In such cases, helping the
animal means helping the owner, and vice versa.

Though some hospitals have rules against vets adopting
a patient, side transactions are tolerated, and they happen
a lot—especially when the owner is unable or unwilling to
cover procedures almost certain to save their pets' lives.
(Nonprofit funding is available for exactly these situations,
and vets always counsel their clients about it.)

Lavotshkin was on duty one night when a big family
brought in a pit bull named Ellie. She'd been hit by a car several days earlier but had seemed fine, so they'd done noth-

ing. Finally, her breathing worsened and they brought her in. When they got Lavotshkin's cost estimate, the owners changed their story: they'd just seen the dog on the street, they said (even though they knew her name). "We don't do it often," Lavotshkin says, "but we just said, 'sign these papers and you lose all rights to the animal.'" Now Ellie shares Lavotshkin's Brooklyn apartment with two other dogs and two cats.

Another of Lavotshkin's dogs is Yogi, who was brought in for heart failure. The day of his scheduled euthanasia, doctors had given him a "last meal" of turkey slices, which he gobbled up so avidly that Lavotshkin decided he just wasn't ready. So she brought him over to her mother's house for a spoiled last weekend, plying him with fried steaks. "That was a year and a half ago," she says. She called in some favors to a cardiologist, who concluded that a pacemaker would save his life. "I actually felt conflicted," she says. "I kept thinking about those hundreds of thousands of other dogs that don't need a pacemaker—they just need a home. But I realized I wasn't taking it away from another dog."

Some excellent veterinarians treat their career as a day job and don't bring it home. Some don't even particularly like animals. But most of them have pets and think of them on the job. When questioned about the gold standard of care, they say, "This is what I would do for my pet"—and they mean it.

In the case of Johanna Ecke, the New Orleans vet who once cried over *Bambi*, being close to a pet helped her understand where her clients were coming from. One of her most devastating cases at the clinic was a dog, Taz, who'd been hit by a car. After five or six days of treatment, he looked stable and healthy enough for surgery on a large fracture. But during the operation his heart stopped, and he didn't make it. Though nothing could have prevented it, the entire hospital was distraught; doctors and techs asked one another, "Is there something else we could have done?" The owners were inconsolable and angry, blaming the vets. Ecke told them what she knew—that they'd done everything they could—and moved on.

Then, a year later, her father's dog Albert had routine knee surgery back in Montana, where she'd grown up. The day Albert was supposed to come home, the kennel informed her father that when they checked in on him, he was dead. "My mom passed away a year before that, and that dog was like my dad's best friend," Ecke says. She called Albert's vets, cursing and grilling them on what might have happened.

"They said they did everything they could," she says. "I was furious!" But then she thought back to her experience with Taz. "They told me what I would have told myself as a vet. And now I was the nightmare client on the phone." Her father's dog was far healthier than Taz when he died, so the two cases were very different. But her personal ties made her better understand "the anger that people can feel when they're grieving." That understanding actually relieved some of her own veterinary guilt. "We want to fix things, make them better," she says, "but as doctors we have to come to grips with the fact that some things are just out of our hands. Some things we just can't fix."

JUNIOR, THE PET WITH the unannounced visit to All Creatures, turns out to be a fat black cat, as affable as the man who brought him in (the owner's boyfriend who appeared sans appointment). Junior has two bacterial infections that are now 75 percent cured, so Dr. Wood orders him to continue with topical applications to the itchy spots. "Okay, Junior, I'm done," she says, before spotting some food stuck in his jaws. "We just need to get the little stuff out of his tooses—Smile for me," says the Baby Voice.

As she brings Junior down for a tune-up with tiny tweezers, Wood checks in on her other patient. "Matty! Oh the Ace kicked in!" she says. Acepromazine puts dogs mostly under before they get gas, and at thirteen, Matty didn't need much, especially for a "snip and three sutures" to remove his cyst. Sam comes down to the basement to share "a really depressing phone call" from an old lady whose cat needs a blood transfusion—and to announce that Bella the rat has arrived. Sam and Wood quibble for a moment over how to add things to "the want list," their prescription drug ordering system. Wood will spend easily 20 percent of the day ordering drugs and another 20 percent writing up medical reports. Now she's hunting for antibiotics. "Our inventory management system leaves something to be desired," she says. "All right, off to see a rat!" And back upstairs we go.

"So this is my little baby Bella," says her owner, a young woman with bright red hair and a brassy voice. Bella is an adorable rat, white-furred with a jacket of pearl gray, who has just started sneezing. "You are very special," says Wood in her baby voice. "Such a lovely creamsicle."

"That's what I call her!" says the owner.

Rats are highly prone to respiratory problems. Bella also needs "a mani pedi," which Wood handles with tiny clippers while Bella emits tiny squeaks. "Oh this is a little ratty scale," Bella's mom remarks when Wood pulls out a pad about eight inches square. "Is she your only rat?" Wood asks. "Wow, you're very lucky." She orders antibiotics and recommends putting Bella in the bathroom during showers. "Nebulizing, just like for kids with colds." It might seem silly to compare a rat to a child, but in the realm of the Baby Voice, all creatures are created equal. The owner thanks Wood. "I'm so happy to have found you," she says before she leaves.

After a couple quick appointments—a rabies shot, canine

dental problems—Wood heads downstairs for Matty's cys-tectomy. There's time for what should be another moment of Zen, but Wood can't manage it. "I'm still worried about this one," she says, gesturing over to the still-sleeping Mil-lie. "The client could sue us, she seems the sort."

Matty is on the floor now, nearly asleep. The table where they'll take out his cyst is for dentistry, her partner, Erica Morgan's, specialty, so Wood has to hunt around Morgan's space for what she needs. "This, do you remember what date is on it?" she asks Lauren, holding up a bottle of fluid.

"No," the tech replies.

"Fine, throw it out," Wood says sharply. "I hate not label-ing things."

Wood says Dr. Morgan recently accused her of "hiding her stethoscope." What actually happened was that Wood had found it "in the middle of a bunch of bloody teeth" and put it in Morgan's mailbox, which Morgan "never checks." I ask how the division of labor is going since the first time we spoke. "About the same," she says. "The partnership's still not good."

The techs haul Matty up on the table by making a gurney out of a towel, nearly dropping one end. Sam comes down with another story (owner on the phone so high he couldn't take instructions) and another short-notice appointment (di-arrheic Yorkie-poo), which Wood decides a tech can handle. The doctor starts to ask Jena for scissors, but stops herself.

"Never mind, I got it," she says. "Years in the bush, years in the bush." She didn't have so much as a table when operating on primates in Liwonde National Park, never mind an assistant to fetch her instruments. Lauren is slightly impressed. "I'm not used to working with doctors who—"

"Do their own shit?" Wood replies. In fact, her self-sufficiency isn't all that rare. I once watched Lavotshkin, the director of a hospital, scoop out and scrub down dog feces in a crate. Whether in a barn or a sterile surgery suite, vets can't always afford to be hands-off. But then, being hands-on is actually a perk of the job. How many human doctors touch their patients out of affection, or cradle them in their gravest hour, or comfort them physically the same way their loved ones would do? Pets are more vulnerable than people, blameless for their ailments, and, for many vets, easier to like.

Matty's positioned on his stomach, legs splayed. Wood pulls out the left one, disinfects the area, and deftly snips off the cyst. "Maybe we saved your life," says Jena in her own baby voice, before cooing over Matty's excellent smell and condition. "Do your owners love you? Do they love you? Usually pit bulls are just gross." Wood has already retreated to the tiny office. "The rat is anemic!" she calls out. She has ten minutes before her next appointment, so she writes up some reports.

Next up is a gentle pug named Ponzu who's been peeing

all over the house. The owner came in after seeing All Creatures on a walk—"it seemed chill and friendly"—vindicating Wood's counting-dogs approach to veterinary real estate. She's reasonably sure Ponzu has a urinary tract infection, but needs to get a sterile urine sample to confirm it. This involves an ultrasound machine, a long needle injected into the bladder, and a muzzle on a dog that's suddenly gotten snappish over the prospect of being pinned down and perforated. "Okay, you're making my life hard," Wood murmurs as she tries to locate the bladder inside the writhing pug.

The next appointment turns out to be far more painful for the owners than for Pickle, the large gray tabby cat they bring in. Pickle had a sore on her lip that seemed to go away a couple of months ago, but now it's back and bigger than ever. The owners, a young Latina and a white man with a handlebar mustache, chat amiably as Wood examines Pickle, but as she gently grips the cat's mouth and sees the smooth, white growth, she grows quiet.

"I'm very concerned," she says. "Now, it could be a couple of things, but it could be cancer." The only other alternative is eosinophilic granuloma, a treatable rash. Wood walks them through the options and, almost without a hitch, turns to her computer to go over costs. "We could just try steroids, but it's gotten worse quickly so I don't want to take a shotgun approach." Sedation, biopsy, and a lab would cost $473 total.

The woman's eyes well up. "We have to do it, right?" They'd been considering getting pet insurance, but Pickle is only two. "It's a preexisting condition now," says Wood. She promises that if things turn out fine, "I will do my best not to diagnose anything else until after you get insurance." The woman thinks for a minute. "She's always picking up things and getting them in her teeth . . ."

"I really don't think it's a dental problem," says Wood, before adding that preoperative bloodwork would inflate the bill by another $120. "Cost being a concern, if you want to make an educated decision not to do that, I'd be fine with that." The owner starts crying again.

"Is cost a concern?" is a standard question in any veterinary setting, asked every time a feverish dog or wobbly rabbit arrives at an ER. The subsequent readout of the options, beginning with the "gold standard" and running all the way down to euthanasia, is the most irksome part of any vet's day. Even in a busy ER, the vet has to agree on a price cap—up to $600—at the end of each initial consultation. Beyond that, the doctor needs to come back to the waiting room and authorize a higher charge. It's a situation with many good outcomes but few that are ideal. And it's a conversation that a vet needs to have in the moment, because the level of care is up to the client.

To the surprise of many a vet-school graduate, improvising treatment plans is a big part of the job. Johanna Ecke remembers taking on a Border collie mix puppy belonging to a group of New Orleans street kids. Duke Jr. turned out to have parvo, a highly contagious, drug-resistant virus that can lead to severe dehydration and far worse. In a shelter it would have been a death sentence.

"Honestly, I looked at them and thought, there's no way they're going to be able to treat this dog," she says. "They live in a commune and it's at least a thousand dollar bill. But they said, 'Look, if you can keep it to X amount and help us in any way you can, we'll do it.' They worked their butts off and paid at the clinic every day." Ecke did her part, donating her time and some medication and bringing down the cost to $850—half what it should have been. Duke Jr. came through. So did his owners and his doctor.

Back at All Creatures, Wood is Baby-Voicing poor Pickle ("Why did you do this?") while settling him into a basement crate. Sam comes running down with a consent form from Pickle's owners. They'd left in a hurry, forgetting to sign it, and when she ran out, she found them at the corner.

"She was hysterically crying," says Sam. "The cat's gonna be fine, though, right?"

"No, probably not," says Wood, as the techs sedate Pickle.

"Where's your food?" Jena asks Wood. It's past three in the afternoon. As in most hospitals, portable lunches are devoured over counters and surgery tables in ten-minute increments.

"I think I ordered some, I'm not sure," says Wood.

"Why don't you go eat, sweetheart?"

"Because if I have food in my mouth when I talk to people . . ."

Several minutes later, we're still waiting on Pickle's bloodwork, which needs to be fed through a slower-than-average machine with a malfunctioning part. "I'm having one of those moments like, where do I start," says Wood. She decides to spend the time writing up some records as fast as she can; she's two days behind and has friends visiting from out of town tonight.

The bloodwork finally arrives, and Pickle's biopsy can proceed. But now she's hiding in her box, and the techs are struggling to bring her out. She's not even close to falling asleep, so they inject another dose of sedative. After she passes out, a tech takes her out and holds her down while Wood uses a sharp cylinder to punch a millimeter-wide hole out of her left lower lip. It takes thirty seconds, but now Pickle is out cold. Five minutes pass, then ten, then twenty. "Come on Pickle, Pickle, up!" says Jena. They take her temperature rectally and see if she stirs. Jena flicks her ears. "Picklesies, wake-ups!" But they mostly leave her be. If the biopsy comes back positive, there'll be plenty of poking and prodding in her future.

Wood paces for a minute, praying for a benign result. "Come on, eosinophilic granuloma, yes, yes," she says, as if she's at a roulette table. Then she's off for her last appointment before Christmas, a beagle that might have eaten some drywall. That pup probably has giardia, and Wood prescribes the usual—a cocktail of antibiotics and probiotics. There's a lot of guessing involved at the general-practice level, at least before the test results come in.

Back downstairs, Pickle perks up, and the techs shout simultaneously: "Pickle!" But by the time Wood comes back, the cat is back at half-mast. "She picked up her head," says Jena, "and said, 'Nah, actually, I hate you all.'" Wood gives her neck a rub: "Eetsh okay."

A week later Wood gets the result. Pickle has eosionphilic granuloma. She needs some topical steroids, but otherwise, she's fine. So is Millie the spayed pit-bull mix, and so is her ornery owner. The Friday before Christmas wasn't an easy day, but by the starkest standard—life or death—it was a good one.

4

SAVE ONE ANIMAL HERE TODAY:
BIG PROFITS AND NONPROFITS

Michael Lund had tried to make it work as a country vet in the middle of the North Dakota oil boom, but he was grossing $50,000 a year and paying $1,000 per month in rent. Finally, he concluded he might as well move somewhere else, somewhere closer to people. "Being on call as a large-animal vet three or four times a week, it's exciting work maybe for a new graduate," he says. "But every time I get called in, it's just more gas, another stop for a quick bite to eat . . ." It was a lonely and inefficient life.

Vets debate whether there are too many of them in small-animal practice, but there's actually a real shortage in low-population areas like North Dakota. In addition to all the obvious drawbacks of the farm-vet lifestyle, there aren't a lot of professionals who want to live so far from an urban center. There is a government program that forgives a portion of loans in exchange for working with livestock in a shortage area; North Dakota offers it, but that wasn't enough to convince Lund to stay.

One of the great benefits of being a vet is that it's highly portable. Lund had friends in New York. He was sociable and young and ready to get to know a big city. He traveled there a few times to interview at New York private practices, but now his lack of an internship was a liability, his clinical experience not applicable. "They're like, who's this cowboy from out West?" But those were temporary obstacles. As in any profession, a wide network of friends and a helpful disposition go a long way. Three of Lund's buddies happened to work at the same New York–area clinic, partly through connections he had made for them. When one of them left, he got the call. He moved to Brooklyn and started working at the practice.

It didn't last. When Lund's one-year contract expired, he left. It wasn't the work, which he took to quickly and happily. He loved working with small animals, and he liked getting to know the clients. But for exactly those reasons, he didn't always push for the highest-cost care. As a mixed-animal vet, "I was used to giving people very honest advice" on more affordable options. He still offered "the best of the best," but was also perfectly candid about the risks and benefits of being less aggressive, and he didn't push tests he felt were unnecessary. "My bosses didn't appreciate people not being convinced to let me spend money right away."

What brought things to a head was a case that came in late one evening—a "very sick dog" with major gas distention, probably due to eating something bad. He referred the owners to BluePearl, a large chain hospital with a branch in Manhattan that housed specialists and an intensive-care unit. "Ten thousand dollars later, the dog is happy and healthy," Lund says. "I see the owner on the street, get an earful for how expensive it was."

A week later he also got an earful from his bosses, who were far less concerned with the excessive cost than with the fact that it was BluePearl that billed it. It didn't seem to matter that Lund's clinic had no overnight facilities and the dog was in the ICU for four days and nights; the owners felt Lund should have kept the dog there.

Lund had a large caseload and was the only doctor on duty on Sundays. "But it was never enough," he says, because he was evaluated on the money made per visit, not the total business he brought in. At the final, fateful meeting with management, he was chided for his low numbers. He asked to see his total record, rather than the per-visit average, and they refused to provide it. "I'm starting to smell that you guys have a different agenda," he remembers thinking. He felt belittled by the implication that he was the practice's weakest link. "I asked them three simple questions: What about my colleagues? Are they feeling like I'm not pulling my weight? 'No, they look up to you.' And what about my clients? 'They seem to love you, no complaints.' And have you had to follow up on my patient care for anything drastic? 'No.' Then I don't know what we have to talk about because I'm doing my job as a veterinarian."

He pauses. "Well, that seems a bit pompous now, looking back. They're running a business, and there's a huge need in urban areas to generate more income." But he still feels they were being unfair and opaque. He wasn't even earning commission. Working on commission creates dubious incentives, but at least it puts the onus on the vet to take the hit if he wants to help out a pet or a client in need.

Lund thinks the pressure does occasionally warp a vet's perspective. The vast majority of cases are basic checkups and diarrhea, not emergencies or dire illness. "More injectable medications in the exam visit, that's the gold standard," he explains. "And that's a good way to get more money." It's also a good way to stay in business.

Of course, reality tends to temper idealism—Lund's included. Vets often convey to clients a diplomatic version of their basic reality: it's expensive to maintain a good practice, with costs ranging from $50,000 for X-ray machines to a living wage for trained technicians. "It's really hard to have cases where your hands are tied," says Ecke. "But my bosses have had to educate me on the cost of running a clinic." She adds that there's a difference between clients who genuinely can't afford care and those who suspect they're being bilked. Many of the latter "don't really understand what we're doing."

Vets start out, generally, in debt, and if those opting for general practice are fortunate, they end up either working for a well-heeled practice or owning one. In either case, financial reality often checks the helping impulse that led them to the profession in the first place. "When I was an employee I could tell clients, 'I'm sorry, I don't have any say in this,'" says Dr. Wood. But as a clinic owner, "What I've been saying more and more is, 'I'm sorry, you're going to need to talk to my practice manager'—who has the very unfortunate role of being the stalwart protection against my charity making us bankrupt."

Complicating these mixed incentives is an inexorable trend in private practice. Like almost every other industry, veterinary medicine is rapidly consolidating in the hands of a few very large corporations. Actually, mostly one corporation: Mars, Inc. Over the past fifteen years, the candy manufacturer invested more and more in pet food and then pet care. By the beginning of 2017 it owned three national chains of hospitals and clinics at various price points: Banfield, a provider of basic, low-cost services located in the back of PetSmart retail stores; BluePearl, a chain of specialty and ER hospitals; and VCA, which buys up and standardizes clinics across the country. BluePearl has around 60 locations, VCA at least 750, and Banfield more than 900.

Corporations own as many as 20 percent of the country's vet practices (still a lot less market concentration than many other industries).

A January 2017 article in *Bloomberg Businessweek* took a sharply critical look at Banfield and VCA, accusing them of pushing profits via "wellness plan" packages and unnecessary booster shots that padded their bills, even as they put pressure on their own doctors to bring in more income. The same motives and methods that allowed Walmart and Barnes & Noble and Amazon to squeeze out smaller, more distinctive mom-and-pop shops are at work in vet care, too. It gets complicated (as it does in human medicine) when such forces begin impacting health decisions. The *Businessweek* piece focused on a few egregious cases in which animals were harmed or franchise owners fired, possibly in the pursuit of greater profit.

The impact on the vet is a little more nuanced. Whether it's a net positive or negative depends on the individual doctor. Lund knows vets who are perfectly happy at chain clinics. They pay relatively well, and their standardized care takes some of the burden off the vet. "My friend who does Banfield out in California, he loves it," says Lund. "He's probably more interested in having a fun weekend than worrying about what his clients think. So I don't get on the negative train for corporate medicine. But it does open up a new can of worms."

The case of one anonymous vet at a suburban VCA clinic gives a sense of the good and the bad; it's also necessary information for prospective vets who want to know what their options will look like when they have to start paying off those debts.

This doctor was employed at a VCA location in one city but needed to relocate for family reasons. "When I found out I had to move and find a job, it was really helpful to be part of VCA," she says. They paid for her travel to interview at new locations. And the chain is hardly Starbucks; there's room for variation. Her new practice turned out to be better managed than the last, but both offered the same, generally high standard of care, with easy access to referral vets in VCA-owned specialty clinics. The company also pays a share of continuing education courses and even residencies—though in return they require multi-year contracts. If you want to learn how to use a fancy ultrasound machine, "You have to give them your soul for two years."

Despite the convenience of her move, the VCA vet still had several concerns, all of them related to the standardization of care. Her salary was negotiated when she arrived, but with the understanding that she was supposed to be making 20 percent of the business she brought in. "Every doctor is compared to every other doctor," she said. She is constantly asked, "'How much did you sell in diets? Why didn't you have more recheck exams?' You should have one lab for every exam. But is that appropriate? They try to tell us it's all about the best medicine, but it's very difficult not to think about money every day."

During a review, the vet was told she wasn't near her 20 percent goal. Neither was any other doctor in the practice, she adds. The location was simply underperforming. "The first six months, I was freaking out: 'I'm twenty thousand dollars in the hole right now.'" They didn't cut her salary, but the idea that she owes her employers money looms over every appointment.

Yet the pressure for more work-ups isn't what bothers her most. The high standard of care is a good thing in many ways. "To a certain point," she says, "good medicine does equate with better production, because shitty medicine is easy—just throw the medication at you without any tests." The real problem, and the reason she says she'll eventually leave, is the lack of autonomy. Like any other big-box chain, VCA (and Mars) pursues efficiencies of scale by negotiating with vendors for bulk orders. As a result, its vets sell a standard suite of products. "I'm worried I'm getting into certain patterns, not thinking for myself," she says. "If you're preferentially selling a medication, maybe it's not something I think is right for that illness. It's definitely impacting our medicine."

There are certain things she can do on the margins: tip owners off to cheaper treatments, or recode certain tests at lower rates. But she resents the idea, which she sees percolating in her clients' minds, that it's the vet pushing the pricey lab work, rather than her boss, or the people in the boardroom. The doctor, too, is feeling the squeeze.

AFTER LUND LEFT THE pushy private clinic, he interviewed at other practices and realized that, wherever he went, he would come up against a mismatch between his own priorities and those of private urban clinics. So he decided to try the city shelter system. He looked up Animal Care and Control in New York (now known as Animal Care Centers of NYC). Over the past five years shelter medicine has seen one of the largest increases in the profession—from 241 practitioners in 2011 to 475 in 2017, according to the AVMA. One big reason might be that shelter medicine itself has become a more pleasant field to work in—cleaner, more efficient, and more humane.

By 2016, the New York system was beginning to live down its reputation for euthanizing large numbers of animals. The "kill rate" went from 60 percent in 2003 to 13 percent in 2016. Still, it was overcrowded and full of disease—difficult work physically, mentally, and emotionally. Lund started out in the ACC's Brooklyn shelter (one of three citywide), and quickly established a regular routine. He would arrive at eight so he could check on the inhabitants before a flood of new arrivals, trying to flag sick animals so they could be treated before they got worse or their disease spread. "You sit down, you put in some of your entries, but now the day has started. Maybe there's a hurt pigeon that just came in and you deal with that." Between animal intakes, treatments, and reports, the team had to perform twenty surgeries daily (mostly neuters and spays). He'd never leave before seven or eight at night.

Which is to say that, for a devoted doctor like Lund, things were going well. Lund was convincing ACC to let him perform more in-house procedures. "There was no reason I couldn't help them with certain surgeries I'd done in North Dakota." It was easier than operating on a cow in a snowstorm, after all. "We had a hum," he says. Then one of his superiors was let go for misfiling a death as euthanasia— an act of laziness that didn't help the shelter's drive to post lower "kill" numbers. It was not, Lund thinks, a grave misdeed. He blames burnout; the superior had been there for well over a decade.

Lund filled in for his former colleague, despite some issues with the management. After the citywide medical director stepped down, he got a shot at a permanent position. Lund was promoted to interim medical director of all three branches, shuttling between his daily Brooklyn routine, "working sixty hours a week in the shelter," and weekly staff meetings and constant email chains.

He was eventually replaced by a full-time director, but stayed on as chief vet. He has nothing but praise for the changes ACC has made over the years. His girlfriend works there happily. He recently pulled a shift there and found it much improved even in the two years since he'd left, approaching a 95 percent live-release rate.

Positive experience aside, "at some point, I was just spent," Lund says. He took a four-month break. He traveled to the Galápagos Islands on a volunteer trip, helping to care for strays. It was there that he realized burnout isn't something you can escape via car or plane—or, as Dr. Wood put it, "there's people everywhere." In the Galápagos, he treated the broken leg of a dog that was fostered by a German researcher. The scientist was eccentric and insisted that the way to treat his pet wasn't a splint shipped from the mainland but a homemade wire contraption constraining its movements. They compromised on an improvised splint made out of cheap aluminum rods. "It's probably got a weird crooked leg now," says Lund. He realized it wasn't just the workload that stressed him out; it was the frequent inability to do what you knew was the right thing.

He had had enough. "I excused myself and I went to the beach for the rest of the day and had a really reflective moment of, 'What's wrong with you?' And every day thereafter, for thirty days, I felt this long, unending beach sunset of just getting a little bit closer to a normal set of parameters." On his return, he decided to join his friend in a startup business in LA—a mobile vet clinic. Eventually, that also floundered over their differing visions, and he was, once again, adrift.

Burnout is a common occupational hazard. One way out of it is to find a safe, slow, stable job—of which there are plenty. Andrew Maccabe, the head of the AAVMC, found the corporate track after a milk surplus forced him out of farm work. He wound up working for the Air Force and the Centers for Disease Control, monitoring the risk of biological warfare and infectious outbreaks. Research jobs in government or industry are secure and lucrative. But a desk job isn't for everyone, and many vets thrive on feeling emotionally invested in animals. As Maccabe himself reports, it's become increasingly clear in recent years that the profession has a responsibility to help its practitioners manage the darker side of the intense love of animals that led them into the field.

Dr. Shirley Koshi's awful story was one of the first to sound the alarm. She began her career in her native India, working for a time with panthers and elephants in the Peshwe Udyan Zoo. She immigrated to the United States, passed the American boards, and practiced in the Northeast for decades. In 2013 she founded her own clinic in the Bronx. But after she adopted a sick cat from a nearby park, Koshi was sued by a woman claiming to be the owner of the cat. Protests and an online harassment campaign ensued, cratering the business she'd spent her life savings to open. In February 2014, she committed suicide.

Her death was followed seven months later by the more baffling suicide of Dr. Sophia Yin. Widely admired by vets and pet owners, Yin pioneered the use of positive reinforcement in animal training, replacing trendy tough-love methods with the use of body language and a treat-dispensing device of her own invention. But her increasing fame seems to have left her feeling overwhelmed, and amid worries about how to juggle her commitments, she spiraled into depression and took her own life.

What could lead these two very different doctors, by all signs devoted and caring and true to their calling, down the same dark road? They were outliers, of course, and making them out to be typical would be sensationalistic, especially as the data on vet depression isn't entirely clear. But these famous cases reverberated across the profession, spawning a conversation that felt, to most everyone, long overdue. Just a few years earlier, in 2010, a British study had concluded that veterinarians were four times as likely to kill themselves as the general population, and twice as likely as medical doctors. It was only the most alarming and concrete of reports across developed countries indicating a heightened risk (though other jobs are correlated with even higher risks). But 2014 was the real turning point, and now the prevalence among DVMs of three related but separate conditions—burnout, compassion fatigue, and clinical depression—comes up regularly in the vet-school classroom as a real and important issue.

VETgirl's Dr. Lee, for example, made a video seminar on suicide available online for free. "It wasn't talked about much when I graduated," she says. But now it's discussed everywhere. Among potential contributing factors, Lee cites the typical vet personality type, "very hard on themselves when they make mistakes," and conditioned to view illness as "weakness." There are also the money concerns, long hours, and the constant exposure to euthanasia, which leads not just to trauma but to increased tolerance of the idea that death is an honorable way to end suffering. Finally, there is the opportunity: ready access to fatal drugs and expertise in administering them.

AAVMC's Maccabe says there really is no conclusive research proving a greatly increased risk of suicide. But the organization is taking burnout and depression seriously. They've persuaded many universities, whose vet schools tend to be far from their parent campuses, to make counselors available on-site. What's new about the phenomenon, he believes, is not its prevalence but the open acknowledgment of it. "These conversations about, 'What is it with these kids today, the trophy generation?' are acts of willful amnesia," he says. "We faced the same stresses, but people kept it to themselves, and that's not healthy either."

From his perspective, the picture is actually improving;

younger vets have more access to education, opportunity, and emotional support than their elders did. For all the talk of oversupply, their unemployment rate is negligible. There's a lot of upside to a profession that's become more varied, more professionalized, more stimulating, and more flexible than it was in the old days of mostly male horse doctors on twenty-four-hour call. Vets may be leaving farms, but there are more places for them to go than there once were: specialty centers for oncology, endoscopy, and animal rehab; government jobs in disease control; conservation centers; corporate offices; IVF facilities; and shelters and nonprofits that are more humane and better managed. If one of those routes begins to feel like a dead end, the solution could be as simple as taking an off-ramp—finding a more fulfilling way to keep doing what you love.

LUND TOOK ONE OF those off-ramps into the ASPCA, finding a job as the staff manager of community medicine in New York. When we met, he was overseeing a rapidly expanding nonprofit primary-care program, providing crucial services not just to animals and pet owners in need, but to vets aiming to feed the altruistic impulses that pulled them into the field. One of the program's linchpins is a mobile spay and neuter program.

In a far northeastern corner of the Bronx, almost as far as

you can go without leaving New York City, sits the Bay Plaza shopping mall. On a frigid day it's a sprawl of concrete and dirty snow, vast and desolate, despite being a ten-minute walk from Co-op City, the largest cooperative housing development in the world. But on this cold morning, along one strip of sidewalk between a Carter's and a Panera Bread, a row of people and pets has been lined up since before 6:00 a.m. Around 7:30 a midsize truck arrives, painted brightly with puppies and kittens and the logo of the ASPCA.

The four-wheeled surgery unit, part of a small fleet in service since 1997, neuters and spays animals for $5 if the owner has proof of public assistance, which all but one of today's clients will. At a private New York clinic the same procedures would cost between $200 and $1,000. The presiding veterinarian arrives at nine. It's almost never the same vet (or the same location) two days in a row. Today's freelance doctor is Njeri Cruse, a thin black woman of medium height with a sardonic laugh and dreadlocks bunched up in two overlapping surgical caps.

"It gets a little crazy here," says Cruse by way of introduction. "Intake is really the most exciting part." She wasn't here for that, in part because it takes two hours to get here from her Yonkers home on public transportation. She's an unusual vet with a career currently composed of shift work, most of it in the service of people with few alternatives and pets who might otherwise end up in shelters (or have litters that do).

The truck holds up to twenty-eight small-to-midsize dogs and cats. Today's menagerie of twenty-three, which owners have left in Cruse's care for the day, includes Bailey and Kobe, Maltese-poodle mixes; Chandler the Boston terrier; and Taffy the "chunky cocker," per Cruse. Shelters often teem with abused pit bulls, but many of the animals here today were bought from pet shops with the best of intentions. Most of their owners care deeply about them, and so does Cruse. A core goal of operations like this is to keep pets with their owners and out of the shelter system. But Cruse also needs to work fast, performing surgeries that take at least a half hour at a clinic like All Creatures in as little as five minutes. Once we get going, Cruse and her team will average five per hour.

The timing of their first incision usually depends on traffic, weather, and the vehicle's temperament. "Sometimes a generator goes out," Cruse says, over the noise of one that's functioning just fine. "So it's like a MASH unit." Opposite the stacked cages is a long counter, the techs' staging area, and in the back is a cube of an operating room—single table, big bright lamp, shelves, and room for two people to stand on either side.

On this particular morning, they can't seem to get started. The delay isn't mechanical or meteorological; it's animal and human. Four female dogs have been flagged as risky—all over five years old and thus borderline geriatric, one of them an obese pit bull in heat and another a bulldog with a runny nose and an ingrown eyelid. None of them have documented pre-op bloodwork, the kind for which Dr. Wood charged Pickle's owners $120. (ASPCA partners can do it for $80.) The owners will have to provide evidence of it, sign releases, or come back another day. But it isn't easy following up with people who may not have flexible jobs.

"So this cat's pretty fractious," Cruse says, ordering an early sedative on a scratchy feline. She asks about bloodwork results on a mini pinscher, which she should have gotten hours ago. She examines Kobe, hunting for an undescended testicle. "This one's spitting in my face. Nice way to start the day." Taffy the chubby spaniel is getting yappy, too. "A lot of them are scared," she says. "It's a completely strange environment, being medicated with a bunch of unusual smells, hands coming at you."

Their owners won't be back until 4:30, after every animal has been operated on and woken up. Cruse feels for the owners, too. About a half hour into her morning prep, a couple knocks on the truck's side door—a man with a bushy beard and a redheaded woman in a puffy coat. Their two Chihuahuas are on the truck—six-year-old Chaya and her son, Titan, who's only a year old but three times her size. Both explode in yaps at the sight of them.

Chaya has no bloodwork, and Cruse explains that they can sign a waiver accepting the risks of geriatric surgery.

"What if you won't be able to wake her up from a nap?" asks the woman, suddenly tearing up.

"If you're not comfortable, there's no pressure," says Cruse. The woman finally decides against it, and scoops Chaya up inside her coat.

"It's an inconvenience for them to have to come back," Cruse says after they leave, "but it's gonna be more of an inconvenience if something goes wrong." A private practice would run plenty of diagnostics—the pre-op gold standard. But here, "we just have us. So I want to minimize the risk."

Her next human visitor huffs up the truck's metal steps a half hour later. She's a little more fractious—more frantic than angry, really. The owner of the runny-nosed bulldog is a large woman in sweatpants and a camouflage jacket. She has a hard time accepting that her pet is too sick for surgery. "Are you the doctor?" she asks Yousuf, one of the techs. (He was a vet in Bangladesh and now he's working toward US certification.) Cruse steps up.

"The problem with his eye," says the woman. "I'm aware of that. Now the upper respiratory—"

"He's wheezing," says Cruse. "And he's got nasal discharge so we don't know what—"

"He's gonna have his eye done and then we have to get the other eye done," the woman says. "We have to get the money in order." She hands over bloodwork results that turn out to be from 2011. "They sent this over, this is supposed to be everything . . . He needs to be neutered, too, because they get cancer and that's gonna be a whole other thing!"

"I'm gonna have to call the practice," says Cruse—but the woman is already talking into her earbuds, evidently on the phone with the dog's actual owner, her daughter. Cruse asks Jeff, another of the techs, about the pinscher's blood-work. "I'm not comfortable going on their word," she says.

Meanwhile the woman is raising her voice at Yousuf. "He's not obese, he's fifty-one pounds!" In fact, obese dogs don't always look overweight to us. "He sleeps all the time— it's in their nature! I feed him twice a day, I don't give him any other food."

"He's a very lethargic dog," Yousuf says.

Cruse chimes in. "The only other way we could do it would be to have you sign a vet exemption." The woman gets back on the phone with her daughter. *"I'm gonna go take him to the doctor. I got—No, no, no, okay, no, stop it. Don't start this crying okay."* Tears start streaming down her face. *"Come on, Jesus Christ."* The woman turns to Cruse. "She is hysterically crying," she says of her daughter.

Cruse tells her she may be eligible for more assistance. "I'll let you know by the end of the day." The owner takes the bulldog to her car. It's well past eleven and we're al-most ready for surgery, so everyone pops out for coffee. On our way out, Cruse sees the tearful owner beside her car and walks over. They talk for another fifteen minutes, after which the owner looks calmer, brighter, knowing that Cruse is doing everything she can to secure affordable care. "There is almost a social-work aspect to the kind of work that we do," Cruse explains later. "The people we're dealing with are facing economic hardship and it's a unique type of medicine we practice. It's not for everyone."

In veterinary care, the greatest sources of stress are inseparable from the most exhilarating moments. For a surgeon it might be a harrowing operation just barely pulled off. For Cruse it's explaining to a frustrated owner with scant money or education that they can make their pets' lives better, as well as their own. "I had a client who smelled like a carton of cigarettes, and her dog was coughing," says Cruse. "It actually had never occurred to her that it was also harming her pet." They agreed together, on the spot, that she would quit smoking for the sake of everyone in her family.

As techs set the stage for surgery, Cruse describes her improvised life. When she isn't on one of these trucks, she could really be anywhere. She's a humanitarian vet for hire—except for a day or two a week at a private practice to pay the bills. She pulls shifts in the back of a Petco near her house (part of a growing chain of "Vetco" clinics, more basic than Banfield). She also works at ASPCA stationary clinics, sometimes in marathon sessions of well over fifty surgeries a day, and sometimes at a new kitten nursery for shelter rescues. There's also another mobile clinic, the Toby

Project. "Tomorrow I'm working in private practice," she says. "Yesterday I was fixing a leak in my ceiling."

Cruse grew up in Clinton Hill, an integrated neighborhood of handsome townhouses in Brooklyn. Her mother was a civil-rights activist in the sixties. As a child, Cruse took in unusual strays: "A turtle named Muhammad, and then a guinea pig with floppy ears. You find everything in Brooklyn. There's actually a really funny picture of me with an alligator that I had," a baby one found in a sewer.

Cruse started an animal rights club in high school. She went on to Hampshire College, a famously free-form school in rural Massachusetts without a lot of science classes. She took most of her vet prerequisites at colleges nearby and wound up gravitating toward horses. After taking more science classes and teaching animal husbandry at the University of Massachusetts, she decided it was time to become a vet.

Cruse applied to two American schools and felt uncomfortable in both interviews. At one southern institution, "I was asked, 'What is that in your hair?' And they said 'Well, you realize that this is a very Christian Republican area. But we do have one Mexican student here.' And I was like, this is lynch town. I cannot go to school here." At the other school, they invited another African American into the interview who wasn't even a vet.

On a lark, Cruse applied to a five-year program at the University of Edinburgh in Scotland—which is accredited by the AVMA. She was accepted within a couple of weeks, and withdrew her other applications. "Everyone else says they had a miserable time in vet school, but that place was magical," she says. In the nineties it was also cheaper than US schools. "A lot of people are in insane debt, but I'm in home debt." She shares a Victorian house with five cats, a ball python, and a mouse. (She keeps the last two very far apart.) Her plan is to retire eventually and "live in a little shack on the bayou, sit in my rocking chair with my cats, and read books."

Before graduating, Cruse spent a summer at New York–area horse racing tracks, and grew disenchanted with equine practice. She diagnosed a horse with lameness before a race, but an older vet overruled her and let the horse run. During the race, its leg "shattered into a million pieces," and of course it had to be put down. That was Cruse's last day there.

Like Lund, Cruse tried private practice and decided it wasn't for her. She found herself offering the gold standard to wealthy clients and euthanasia to the poor. So she headed to shelter medicine—first the ACC, where, also like Lund, she was briefly the medical director. It was still the bad old days there. "The first day I walked into a kill shelter, I was in tears," she says. "And my mom said, 'You save one animal here today, you can say you've done something to make a difference.'" Nonetheless, she, too, burned out. After nine years, "I was like, I've got to get the hell out of there."

———

BY THE TIME THE techs are pulling cats out of their cages, it's 11:30. The next four hours will follow an order dictated by surgical logic. Six male cats will come first: those neuters are quick and bloodless and only lightly sedated, because for some reason male cats are prone to anesthetic complications. "They just like to run into the light," says Cruse. Then come the female cat spays, more invasive than the neuters and slower to wake than the dogs. Cruse's first dog will be a male red-and-black sixty-pound boxer. He'll need to be the most awake because he might have to walk home; many owners in the Bronx don't have cars. Then they'll spay the labor-intensive but fast-rising female dogs and end with the much easier small male dogs.

The assembly line starts up quickly. A tech shaves and catheters the two sleepy male cats on the counter and takes a noisy whirring vacuum to their fur. Another tech lifts each one in turn onto the slim metal surgery table, intubates him, clips a vital-sign tracker to his tongue, and Cruse begins. She makes a quick slit in the scrotum, pulls on the testicles, twists, clamps, cuts, and twist-ties. (Male cats don't need stitches.) She dispatches the six of them in a little over a half hour, talking the whole time.

Cruse does pretty well financially. Compared to other doctors, "It looks like I make more initially," she says, "until quarterly tax time, and then it gets tricky with the write-offs." The ASPCA pays surgeons on a points system that can rival the hourly ER rates on a great day, "but in terms of budget, you really only plan for the minimum and hope for more."

Finally, the pinscher's bloodwork comes in—through another tech's phone. (Cell coverage is spotty at Bay Plaza.) "Okay, min pin good to go!" she says. But now it's time for the female cats, which are on the heavier side today, slowing down the work. "I just took out subcutaneous fat," she says on the first one, throwing a lumpy mass into a bowl. "Now I'm hunting for uterus." It's a short treasure hunt. Soon she's disconnecting the uterine horns, two long tubes capped with tiny ovaries, then sewing up the vessels and snipping off the tubes.

She wipes her brow and pulls on her mask, asks a tech to adjust the lamp: "It burns my brain." It's below freezing outside but the back room requires a cooling fan. The hardest thing, she says, is "when you run into emergencies and you're on an island, having to work on your feet calmly and effectively." Every couple months, a truck surgeon will have to perform an "autotransfusion," running a pet's own blood through a filter and pumping it back in. "You wouldn't normally see that in a private practice." The mortality rates on the truck are below 0.1 percent. On this relatively drama-free day, the mood is light, full of inside jokes. Cruse and her techs look like happy warriors on the front lines of the battle to keep pets in loving homes.

Cruse's flexible schedule leaves her time to pursue strange and varied hobbies. "I wrote something on the history of vampires in Africa—oh, do we have a cyst?" she says, probing one cat. She participates in "root work," a system of homeopathic healing based on Afro-Caribbean traditions. She's organizing a symposium at Hampshire on "human-animal spiritual bonds and relationships." She's written an article on an indigenous tribe's dentition for the *Journal of Paleopathology*. "Absolutely boring," she says. "The weird things you do when you're vetting." Cruse gestures at the techs. "They're happy you're here because they get a break from me. Sometimes we play club music because it makes us feel like we're going out."

The first dog, the large boxer, is hauled up on the table. He's nowhere near the biggest dog she's squeezed onto this two-foot-wide metal slab. "I spayed one Great Dane on the truck—and that was it for me." Today's workload is on the light side. "We lost a lot of time this morning, but volume-wise—it could have been one of those days when you have twenty-eight animals and then they hold a bucket down for all your tears."

After neutering the boxer, it's time for the female dogs. The first one is in heat, which engorges the organs with blood. "She's got a nice juicy one," Cruse says, poking at the uterus. "Don't get queasy! Did you ever watch the show

Dexter? I love horror. I used to cut my bear up and sew it back together, and my mother said, 'She's either gonna be a vet or a serial killer.' I took the better of the professions." She flashes a demonic smile.

Female dogs are particularly fatty. That means more poking around, and more room for error. At last, Cruse snips off an ovary and shows it to me up close. It resembles a chickpea, only smaller and with two creases. "All of that work, just to get to this! Now you feel my pain on these fat girls." Off in the front room, the cats are stirring on the counter. In the far crate, the boxer makes his first waking-up noises, which sound like the snores of a cartoon ghost.

Cruse works to suture the dog's incision with care, avoiding an enlarged spleen. Has she ever ruptured one? "First spay I did. I was so enthusiastic, too!" During her first surgery in school, she asked a teacher what might happen if your clamp were to slip and open up a vessel. "And so she let go, and the animal just filled up with blood. And I was like, 'Oh bleep bleep bleep!' And then she taught me how to handle it. Afterward she said, 'I'd rather you get over the fear now, when you have me, than to have it happen in practice, because that's how you lose animals.'" She's never lost one during surgery.

After all those fat females, the three dog neuters are a breeze. Back in the crates, the other animals are stirring in different stages of arousal. The boxer's ghostly flutter harmonizes with whimpers and squeaks. Cruse quickly dispatches Kobe, the Maltipoo with the hidden testicle—found and excised. The other Maltipoo, still wearing his doggie jacket, goes even more quickly. Cruse and Jeff pass the time with stories of clients from hell.

Jeff says he was once threatened with murder. "When the cops go on raids and confiscate the dogs, [the owners] come right out of jail and to the ACC," he explains. He also had a client come back to the ASPCA truck in a rage, insisting the surgeon had removed his dog's nipple and demanding its replacement. Cruse says the Vetco at Mount Vernon is "like a lawless nation. I had somebody toss a table on me and the technician, who was pregnant."

Despite those rare moments for Cruse, which at least make good stories, the job is exciting and it's essential—and maybe exciting because it's essential. "You've already seen a couple of clients cry today," she says. "Any time you have a population that waits at five in the morning to get their pets done, they love them." Finally it's coming up on 4:00 p.m., "when we shake the animals down and say, 'You've got to get up, your time is over!'" And then the owners arrive, weary from work, relieved and grateful.

5

THE SPECIALISTS, PART ONE: CRITICAL CASES

The ASPCA's expansion is making Lund feel, once again, overextended. Unsure of his future as a manager, he anticipates another bend in the road—not a burnout, but a change—and has been preparing accordingly. In 2016 he applied to nine programs for a residency in pathology, without success. So now, in 2017, "I'm back to the drawing board."

Lund's growing interest in pathology—the study of not only individual causes of death but also epidemics—is in part a consequence of his shelter work, a ground-level crash course in stemming the spread of disease. But it also connects him to that first passion of so many idealistic vets: wildlife medicine. After volunteering at the Bronx Zoo, Lund was keen on their joint pathology residency with Cornell's wildlife center. But he was competing with both star interns and applicants with years of published research under their belts. "Was I the best candidate?" he asks. "Absolutely not." (He's probably being a little hard on himself;

the year he applied, there were three applicants for every residency position in the country. That's why so many specialists wind up doing a second internship.)

Residencies can be a gamble—high-risk (at low pay) for high-reward. "The sky's the limit with some positions," says Lund, "but you need to be the best and the brightest and know people to get those positions." Still, it's a way forward. "I don't see a twenty-year trajectory here," he says of his current job. "I see a couple years to learn something and then get on to the next thing."

More and more vets are getting on to the next thing. The number of board-certified specialists—in fields ranging from oncology to dermatology but especially in critical care, surgery, and internal medicine—has risen steadily in recent years. There are 8 percent more board-certified specialists than just three years ago, outpacing the total increase in vets by 35 percent. And compared to five years ago, 48 percent more AVMA members today report working in referral or specialty medicine.

The trend toward specialization runs in tandem with another; vet care is becoming more and more like human medicine. Less than one-third of MDs work in general practice, and that makes sense to us, even though they already specialize in only one species. They don't have to treat a rat, a chicken, a rabbit, and a dog on the same day.

There's less demand for referral animal health care for the simple reason that fewer people are willing to spend money on it, but more and more vets are choosing to test that status quo.

One reason vets do decide to specialize—especially the many who try general practice first—is the desire to trade breadth for depth. "I would rather know a lot about a little," says Jesse Terry. In 2016 he completed a residency in surgery, becoming the fourth vet surgeon in Utah.

As in human medicine, there's a specialty for every veterinary personality. Surgeons tend to be confident, comfortable with giving orders and making high-stakes decisions. The worriers and studiers go for internal medicine. "I like to take my time, think things through, really delve into a case," says Jenn Harrison, a third-year internal-medicine resident at Penn. And then there is emergency and critical care, encompassing the ER and the ICU.

"Maybe the more ADD types like emergency," says Lavotshkin. "I can fix this and then I get the next one and you go!" But the enemy of the emergency room isn't focus: it's neurosis, which can lead to panic. "You quickly see among your interns who comes in very early just to be as prepared as possible, and then is a nervous wreck until the next rotation," she says. "Those are the people that like general practice."

Critical-care vet resident Brittany Sylvane puts it a little more bluntly. "General practice is boring," she says. "It's a great job for some people. You can have continuity of care, a relationship with people, and it sounds like a very nice job. I personally like a little more excitement."

DR. SYLVANE IS ONE of twenty-nine fortunate residents at the Animal Medical Center, where a recent residency opening netted one hundred applicants. The hospital occupies an eight-story building overlooking the Queensboro Bridge in Manhattan, and it houses experts in every specialty you could imagine, operating not as separate fiefdoms but as an interdependent system devoted to total animal care. If that system had a mouth, it would be the second-floor emergency room.

On a slower-than-average Monday, Dr. Nili Uhrman is the resident in charge of the ER. A petite woman with sharp features and a habit of speaking incomprehensibly fast, Dr. Uhrman is juggling fourteen cases by the time lunch rolls around. But she's not taking lunch. She's at one of three exam tables in the spacious emergency room, using a kind of caliper to pinch the vertebrae of a scraggly Yorkie named Tee who can barely move his hind legs.

"His presentation is pretty consistent with a herniated disk," she says. "The only way to diagnose it is with an MRI, and then it's a surgical emergency." She'll need to go over the options with the owner, currently in the waiting room, "but let me just look at this one other cat."

"Oh, Beaux," says Claudia, a technician on duty. Beaux is an uncommon breed of cat, a Nebelung, with a long, luxurious coat of gray. She came in last night vomiting but was sent back home for the night. That was a mistake, Dr. Uhrman realizes. "Is that a string under your tongue?" She already suspected a swallowed foreign body, and now it's confirmed. Quickly she performs a possibly life-saving procedure: she snips the string with scissors. If it was still attached to whatever is in her intestines, it's now been released, relaxing the digestive tract. "This cat will definitely need to go to surgery. But we'll go ahead with the ultrasound."

Dr. Uhrman checks in briefly with another stomach case, a sore ten-year-old beagle named Huck. Then she readies poor paralyzed Tee for his MRI, and finally we're heading down the corridor, through swinging doors, into a warren of fourteen exam rooms—first come, first served. "Owners of Tee," she calls out into the waiting room. We're joined by a woman in smart athletic wear.

"Let's steal this room," Uhrman says, pulling a metal sliding door. Then she asks for Tee's story. The owner noticed yesterday that Tee was wobbly on his hind legs. Her primary-care vet advised a visit to the ER the night before, but Tee improved a little and she decided against it. By morning, though, he couldn't get up.

Uhrman says that lines up with what she observed in the ER. On a notepad, she does a rough drawing of a spinal cord pushed from below by two errant disks. Depending on how many disks are actually affected, the surgery could take anywhere from four to eight hours.

"Do you think I should have taken him in last night?" the owner asks, eyes welling up.

"It's hard to say," says Uhrman. "Right now his prognosis is good, but this is certainly an emergency surgery."

"I'm just so upset, is there something I could have done differently?"

"Some animals are just predisposed," says Uhrman, kindly. The owner wipes away a tear, and Uhrman waits a beat.

"All right, so now we need to talk about the estimate—the fun part," says Uhrman, in a way that somehow cheers her client up. She ballparks a $5,800 bill. The owner has insurance—a rarity even at a full-service hospital like this.

"So that went well," Uhrman says as we return to the ER. "We're good to go," she tells Jen, the tech who ferries animals from the waiting room. Then she sees Kelsey Goode, an intern on ER duty who's currently using a crude ultrasound device to "flash" Huck, the aching beagle. "Did you get a blood pressure on that cat?"

"Uh, yes," Goode says. "Zelda, she will be back after her chest RADS [X-ray]." Opposite the ER, in the radiology room, is a much more sophisticated ultrasound machine hooked up to a monitor the size of a large desktop screen. Beaux, the string-swallowing Nebelung, is being held down by a tech on a concave cushion. Seated behind them, ultrasound wand in hand, is Anthony Fischetti, the hospital's head of diagnostic imaging and radiology.

"Cats like to eat string," says Dr. Fischetti, roving his wand across Beaux's shaved belly. "Right there. See that shadowing line going through? Oh boy. You're hurting." The shifting grays of the ultrasound screen resolve into sinuous guts, with a faint straight line running across. "It usually lodges up against the PDJ," he says. That would be the pyloroduodenal junction—the same area Dr. Elisha Frye was hunting for, only with her hand, when that sick, tired cow lay down.

Though there's "really severe bunching," Fischetti says, pointing to where the gut now resembles a ghostly scrunchie, the string is now advancing through the intestine—a good sign. It could heal on its own, "but if this were my own cat, I wouldn't want to wait. I think it should go to surgery."

Fischetti, who has the casual posture and amiable smirk of a cool high-school history teacher, has been here fourteen years, if you count his residency. Like a lot of doctors here, he came in as a student and never left. His particular personality seems suited to radiology: "It's the fountain of youth. I really like anatomy, and it has a very quick turnaround—a lot of cases over a short period of time, and a lot of puzzles."

Back in the ER, Dr. Uhrman is taking a few moments to make progress on paperwork—from which even ER vets are not spared. Three computers sit in a corner, at least two of them occupied at all times by doctors typing furiously. Between reports, Uhrman recounts her own history for me. "My mom wanted to be a vet but could never go through with it because of the euthanasia," she says. "So she probably brainwashed me." As an undergrad at the University of Florida, Uhrman attended a presentation from Ross University, the giant for-profit Caribbean school. "I thought it was so cool," she says. "I only applied to a couple of state schools," but her GRE scores weren't so high. She enrolled before Ross was fully accredited, but the AVMA gave it the nod "while I did my clinics, thank God." Ross's graduation standards are said to be as high as those of American schools. (More are admitted, but more flunk out.) Uhrman loved it at Ross, but the debt has almost made her rethink her career. "That's how crushing it is."

A few feet away, Claudia holds down Huck the beagle while Dr. Goode takes blood. "Come on, sugar pop, don't be nervous," Claudia says. "Who's being the bravest boy in the whole wide world?"

"Claudia, I have another career choice for you," says Jen. "You could be a doula." Goode, meanwhile, is attending to Zelda, a cat with leukemia and liver issues. "We can do supportive care but once they have clinical signs, that's pretty much the end. I'm going to talk to Zelda's mom and see what she wants to do." I move to follow but Uhrman stops me. Zelda will likely be euthanized, so it won't be an easy conversation. Working in critical care entails wearing many faces, one after the other. It puts vets at risk for compassion fatigue—not depression but indifference due to overexposure. One minute you're tearfully performing euthanasia and the next you're cooing at a perfectly healthy kitten.

Tee is ready to be taken for his MRI, but first a vet has to hose him down; he had an accident in his crate. A few minutes later, Jen race-walks in with a soft cat carrier—a genuine emergency. Yoshi, the squirrely gray shorthair inside, has a fever of 105.7 and a heartbeat of 280. "That's okay, sugar, that's okay," says Claudia, holding him down on the table as Dr. Uhrman takes a look. "All right," Uhrman says to herself, "it's one year old, does it have something infectious and terrible?" They roll out an EKG machine, fiddling with the knobs. The clothespin-like clamps keep slipping off Yoshi's chest, and the readout is hard to decipher, so they call in a cardiologist, Dr. Dennis Trafny. He discovers palpitations and prescribes a beta blocker. As in so many cases, the proximity of specialists turns out to be critical.

Soon afterward, Jen brings in Loki, a woozy old dog with diabetes. Uhrman reads something that looks like a receipt but is actually a printout from a lightning-fast bloodwork machine—certainly much faster than the one Dr. Wood was waiting for at All Creatures. Loki has a pH that "you learn in school is not consistent with life," says Uhrman. "But we see levels that are crazy sometimes." He's in full diabetic crisis.

Loki will have to spend at least a couple of nights in the ICU across the hall. When I visit him there later, Dr. Sylvane offers a tour of the crates, accessorized with IVs and ventilators. "This cat's in kidney failure, this dog has an ear infection that went into its brain . . . this cat's in heart failure, this dachshund had a splenectomy," says Sylvane. Loki "is probably the sickest in the room, getting tons of treatments to get him through the first twenty-four hours." This is the "critical care" side of Sylvane's residency, and also one of the most expensive services. Three nights in intensive care can cost up to $5,000. What's true of the ICU is true of all specialties; their benefit to both vets and pets depends on the owners' ability and willingness to pay.

Back in the emergency room, Beaux is out cold and ready to be prepped for surgery. A new technician, Alla, has started her shift. She reports that Yoshi's fever is down to 103.6. She's fond of aphoristic statements about her profession, such as, "You go into this because you want to work with animals. Then you find out dogs don't have credit cards."

Dogs whose owners have credit cards are the ones that specialists work with. It's no accident that Jesse Terry, the fourth animal surgeon in Utah, works in the wealthy ski town of Park City. "Specialists are there for the 5 percent of the population that is looking for the most advanced possibilities out there," he says. What drove Njeri Cruse from general practice to shelter work is exactly what drove Terry in the opposite direction, toward specialized care for the better off. General practice meant treating animals differently depending on their owners' credit limits. In specialty medicine, "you don't have to do that." Where money is no object, it isn't an issue either.

AN ENORMOUS ROOM AT the end of AMC's second-floor hall, lined with seven big tables under lamps and IV racks, looks like an operating area but turns out to be the surgical prep room. Small teams of techs painstakingly attend to all the preliminaries that were handled in five minutes on the counter of Njeri Cruse's ASPCA truck. Beaux spends more than a half hour being sedated, catheterized, shaved, and intubated. On a neighboring table, Tee is being prepared for his much longer spinal surgery. His MRI revealed four slipped disks.

Beaux's surgeon, Dr. Pamela Schwartz, emerges from a back room. She heads one of AMC's three general-surgery teams, each of which handles roughly twenty operations per week. The surgical suites might as well be on a different planet than the barn where Elisha Frye fished around in a cow's stomach. Everyone attending must wear scrubs, a mask, a cap, and booties. An instrument table lined with sterile blue paper cannot be touched by anyone but the surgeon and her assistants. Doctors put on their gloves by using the ends of their gown sleeves as pincers, flipping the gloves over in a delicate choreography so the exterior never makes contact with any skin.

"Since we're a teaching hospital, we have to teach people the right way," says Schwartz. Out in the real world, "there're corners you can cut." The operating theater is hard to distinguish from a human OR—except maybe by the size of the table (which could still fit a small person). It does, however, seem to lack a sound system for Schwartz's iPhone, which blares upbeat hip-hop from its own tinny speaker while she works.

First, she goes over medications and instruments with the tech on duty and runs casually through a set list of questions.

"This is Beaux. He's here for a linear foreign body. Did he get pre-op antibiotics?"

"Yep."

"How's he doing on pre-op anesthesia?"

"He's doing wonderful."

"Great. Can we raise the table, please?"

"No problem."

"We're gonna get started if that's okay with you."

"Yep."

"Okie dokie, we're cutting."

Schwartz is another AMC lifer. She did her internship here fourteen years ago and never left. "What appeals to me about surgery? It's very challenging, no case is ever the same, I still get to learn and do new things. And it's never just surgery. There's oftentimes a medicine or oncology component."

It's also unpredictable. For all the fancy imaging available at AMC, Schwartz won't know what to expect until she cuts into Beaux. "Sometimes we make one incision or multiple incisions," she says. "Sometimes you have to remove intestines." Cutting through the fat layer, she checks the organs one by one. "Liver looks good. Little pancreas is right there, it's fine. And the kidney—he's so fat I'm not gonna be able to see it, but I can feel it, it's fine."

Schwartz never really wanted to be anything other than a vet, she explains while she works. She briefly considered human medicine, but "dogs and cats are cuter." Finally, she lays out Beaux's digestive tract for inspection. Two bulges are visible in the small intestine. "So it's probably tethered," she says as she investigates. "Yup, I can feel string, so if I pull this, it gets more bunched up." She turns to Lisa, the intern observing. "So what side, ideally—where are you gonna make your incision?" she asks, tracing her finger down the length of the obstruction. "Here, here, or here?"

Lisa suggests the end closest to the rectum and Schwartz agrees in principle. Better to run in the direction of digestion. "But I'm gonna push it back to see if we could make just one cut, and make it nicer." She squeezes one lump of string through the intestine about four inches down, like toothpaste through a wrinkled tube, until what she has is one loopy mass. She clamps around the new bulge and cuts once.

Perseverance is among a surgeon's greatest assets, and it's what got Schwartz to this table. She was a technician for two years while applying unsuccessfully to vet school. She had worked her way up to surgery tech, and liked what she saw. So did her bosses, who wrote her recommendations. She only got into Ross University and Atlantic Veterinary College, on Prince Edward Island in Canada. Schwartz attended the latter.

"People looked down on it," she says. "But it really doesn't matter where you go to vet school because they can't teach you how to be a vet. It gives you a foundation, and then you learn to be a vet your first year out of school." After graduating, she was rejected by every residency she applied to for two years in a row before getting in on the third try. "But for me there was really nothing else that I was interested in doing."

Gingerly, Schwartz pulls out a hard mass of string and other digested matter. "Oh that's nice. Wooh! Stinky." It's no longer green like the piece Uhrman clipped from under Beaux's tongue. "The nice thing so far is that the vasculature wasn't compromised. Sometimes blood vessels die off and you have to resect it"—cut a piece out and reattach the living ends. "Boring is good sometimes," she adds, while suturing the small cut in the intestine.

Schwartz has no problem generalizing about her fellow surgeons: "Big personalities. You can't be wishy-washy. And when things get bad, I get very hyper-focused and calm." She counts up the gauze she used inside, to make sure she left none behind inside the cat. The count is off because the techs threw some used pieces away, and she warns the attending tech about it—firmly but calmly. She can't find anything else, inside or out. The gauze is marked to be visible on X-ray, so she orders a post-op X-ray.

For all of Schwartz's confidence, she isn't completely without regrets. "I would have told my younger self to not work as hard as I worked," she says while stitching up Beaux's outer incision. "To work on more of a life-work balance earlier on." Prioritizing your career above all else is "easy to do in a place like this, where our clients are extremely demanding." But she's realized that time for oneself is important, too. "You want to help," she says, "but you can't do it all."

USUALLY THERE'S AN EVENING rush at the ER, but tonight a powerful rainstorm has minimized emergencies—or at least the activities that lead to emergencies. There's only a smattering of arrivals: a dog throwing up bile, probably treatable with a two-week course of antacid; a white cockatoo with a sore under his wing; and a pit bull in the waiting room with a giant scrape on his forehead, an angry gash under his eye, and an even angrier disposition.

"That dog is aggressive, and I have a pit bull," says Alla, the voluble tech. She saw the animal from afar and turned right around. This intake duty falls to an intern, Jacob Klos, a thin Midwesterner with an overgrown buzz cut. He brings a muzzle along as we hunt for an available exam room big enough to give the dog a little space. Klos is currently awaiting replies to his residency applications, and already having an edgy week. "I sometimes feel—often feel—that I made a mistake doing this career. I enjoy it but it's a lot of hours and not very good pay." He's heard the spiel about millennials like him—"how we feel like we deserve things"—from older vets, but that generation didn't work any harder; they just had lower debt.

"I worked eighteen hours yesterday," he says. He caught a

case ten minutes before the official end of his shift, at midnight, and spent an hour unblocking a cat's urinary tract. Then he had four hours of paperwork. He was back here at 11:00 a.m., and now he needs to handle an angry pit bull.

After one look at Leo, the snarling beast, straining against a leash held by a rough-looking father and son in the waiting room, Klos hands them the muzzle at arm's length.

"Sorry, a little vicious," says the father, once Leo's been wrangled into the exam room. "He's a very . . . good-looking dog," Klos says. He worries that stitching up the gash under Leo's eye might deform the eyelid, and he'd have to use sedation. "He's not going to want us to be near his face."

"Yeah, he's got an attitude now, he's aggravated," says the son.

"I'll have to ask a second opinion," says Klos, trying to make nice with Leo, who snarls. "Okay. Well, I'm gonna let her know." We leave quickly through the back door. "I was hoping Nili would be back here," Klos says when we return. But instead of Dr. Uhrman he finds her evening relief, Dr. Andrea Trafny.

Dr. Trafny had a slightly circuitous path to the ER. She graduated from Parsons School of Design and spent a few years as an art teacher. "Then someone told me it was really hard to be a vet, and I said, 'I can do it!'" While teaching, she spent three years fulfilling her pre-vet requirements at Hunter College. Her plan B was human medicine; plan

C was dentistry. From her point of view, it's easier to have tried something else than to rush into animal medicine. Her husband, Dr. Dennis Trafny, the AMC cardiologist, barreled through vet school on an early-decision program, "and then he had to find himself as a person."

The female Dr. Trafny is in charge of the ER schedule. Each doctor spends two months in one of three eight-hour shifts—day, evening, and overnight—usually one week on and one week off. The unusually quiet evening allows the day shift doctors to finish up paperwork. One intern, Stephany Chang, is ten minutes away from seven o'clock, the official end of her shift. After that, she'll still have to finish her reports, but she won't have to take any cases.

"You're gonna get your last case at 6:52," Claudia teases Dr. Chang.

"I'm gonna be so pissed," says Chang. "What I need to do is barricade that door."

"Sometimes they'll gamble with each other," says Andrea Trafny. "Something easy will come in at 6:55, like bloody diarrhea that's stable, and you watch them struggle with whether to take it. 'Do I gamble that nothing else will come in?'"

"Always take it!" says Klos, still disgruntled over yesterday's midnight cat. Dr. Trafny agrees: "Always take the bloody diarrhea."

Trafny came to AMC as an intern in June of 2007, met

her husband here, and never left. "I just don't even know anything else." Alla chalks up AMC's high retention rate to the quality of medicine. She talks about innovations at the hospital, particularly in the field of interventional radiology. "There are only two doctors in the world that do that," Alla says, exaggerating a bit. They're both at AMC, and like the Trafnys, "they're both also married to each other."

6

THE SPECIALISTS, PART TWO: THE PLATINUM STANDARD

One flight up from AMC's emergency room, behind a door marked INTERVENTIONAL RADIOLOGY & EN- DOSCOPY, Drs. Chick Weisse and Allyson Berent start the day with morning rounds, a ritual familiar to anyone who's worked in a human hospital. Gathered around them are about a dozen doctors and techs and three visiting vets from Michigan, Boston, and Italy. Weisse, wearing an athletic sweater and tan Adidas in lieu of scrubs, runs the show.

"All right. Wendy!" he calls out, reading a dog's name off a large lined whiteboard, a set of rows and columns filled in with tiny multicolored bits of medical information. An intern presents the case: "Four-year-old female spay shih tzu, history of cystolithiasis," she says, meaning an obstructive growth in the bladder. "The owner was pretty intent on speaking to a veterinary urologist and when she found out that didn't exist, she was told she may want to speak with you."

Wendy's owner is dithering about the visit. "Let's see if she shows," says Weisse. "We don't want to waste any time. Dignan!" Another intern describes moderate obstruction in the dog's vulva. "It was completely stenotic!" Weisse interjects— fully blocked. "You opened up the vulva and there was basically a sheet of tissue." On it goes, with Weisse and Berent calling out names, diagnoses, and interruptions: an exercise designed to glean information, plan the day's care, and test residents and interns on their knowledge and judgment.

None of these are easy cases. Geriatric problems alternate with congenital deformities. Most of them would have been incurable, or subject to high-risk surgeries, a decade ago, and still would be today if not for interventional radiology. The growing subfield is at once exceedingly complex— nimbly adapting minimally invasive surgery to the specific needs of small animals—and conceptually simple. As one tech puts it, "We close up things that are open and open up things that are closed."

Weisse and Berent are married with three young daughters. "I constantly think about what they're going to do," Weisse tells me later, while the team breaks for lunch. Life and work are inseparable for the couple, who like to say they spend twenty-three and a half hours of the day together. Their first collaboration was not a child but a surgery that made veterinary history—and may also have been the nerdiest meet-cute of all time.

Weisse has the affable cockiness of a finance bro, which is what he once wanted to be. He grew up in New Jersey "in the eighties, with investment bankers driving around in limos. No one knew what an investment banker did but everyone wanted to be one." Hoping to end up at the World Bank or the Federal Reserve, he graduated from Boston University and was on his way to a master's in economics when he had an epiphany: "This is boring." He started working nights as a veterinary tech, handling emergency phone calls on his own, learning on the fly with four medical books spread open on his desk. After taking pre-vet post-bac classes at Harvard, he got into the University of Pennsylvania vet school on his first try.

Before he went, Weisse didn't even know that veterinary specialties existed. But Penn, the most urban of vet schools, was an exhilarating crash course in critical care. "You'd see a lot of dogs hit by cars, gunshot wounds, crashing and burning stuff," says Weisse. "So as an intern, you would do surgeries." He took to it quickly, even though he doesn't consider himself a natural. "One of the things I liked about surgery was that I was afraid of it, which is why I wanted to get good at it."

He stayed at Penn as an intern and then a resident. Early in his residency Weisse came across a dog with a collapsing trachea that was too deep in its chest for conventional surgery. He knew that in similar cases, a few vets had tried using stents—small tubes inserted via catheters through tiny incisions, usually to unblock vessels. In human medicine, they're much safer than open-heart surgery and other invasive procedures, and usually implanted with the guidance of real-time X-ray videos (hence the term "interventional radiology"). Penn wasn't doing it for pets, though; it was relatively new, and animal care always lags behind the human "gold standard." So Weisse called the university's human hospital.

Doctors put him in touch with a human IR specialist who loved pets and offered to help. Their friendship resulted in a special post-residency fellowship for Weisse, during which he spent one day a week watching human procedures, visiting patients, and observing rounds—witnessing a model for the human-style department he coleads today. Animal IR was becoming a bigger and bigger part of Weisse's life by the time Allyson Berent arrived at Penn.

Unlike Weisse, Berent knew she wanted to be a vet from the age of eight. But she was also driven, like him, more by curiosity and ambition than by a consuming love of pets. "I'm not a crazy animal person," she says. "I'm a kid person. I don't wear necklaces of my dog's ashes. Every one of my clients loves animals more than I do." (Weisse keeps a small dog-shaped trinket over his desk, a gift from an owner made with the fur of her own euthanized dog. It's a funny talisman, but also a reminder of his clients' devotion.) What actually made Berent want to be a vet was that her friend's sister wanted to be one, and when she shared her new plan with her third-grade teacher, "she told me, 'You know, it's really hard to be a vet.'" That was just the push she needed.

"She went to a little school up north," says Weisse, joking about Cornell in the same way that Harvard grads talk coyly about "studying in Boston." Like Catherine Wood, she got both her bachelor's and her DVM there. Along the way, her studious perfectionism led her to internal medicine. "I had a thirst for more details, and I don't like passing things off to people." At the University of Minnesota, where she later interned, Berent was frustrated by the limitations of conventional surgery. One of her first cases was a Yorkie with a tracheal collapse, a poor candidate for surgery. Berent approached the surgery department about stenting. "They told me stents don't go well," and they went ahead with conventional surgery. "It was a horrible death, and I regretted it. So every time I had a case when I was told there's no good option, I would look at what they do on humans."

The following year, Berent was in the first week of her internal-medicine residency at Penn when she came across exactly such a case—the one that brought Weisse and Berent together. "His name was Joey, I remember very clearly," she says. The dog couldn't urinate because of a tumor blocking his urethra. Joey's cancer was incurable, but Berent wanted to do what she could for his quality of life. So she approached her superior with a question: If stents could be put in animals' airways, why not run one through a catheter in their urinary tract? "She said, 'I don't know, but there's somebody here who does tracheal stenting. Why don't we ask him?' That was Chick." Weisse was happy to help; he suggested a different stent and put the funding together for the surgery. "We wound up putting a stent in the dog's urethra, and Joey peed on the table," Berent says with a proud smile. It was the first time that the procedure had ever been done.

Beginning with Joey, Berent was particularly interested in endoscopy, which focuses on the digestive and urinary tracts. A loyal client funded a fellowship for her to spend more time working with Weisse and observing procedures at the human hospital. Eventually, the couple had so many cases they created their own practice within Penn. When it grew large enough, they explored running a separate program. AMC made the best offer. In 2009, the hospital launched a $2.5 million renovation to build their department—about half of it for a surgery suite large enough to contain a state-of-the-art fluoroscopy (live X-ray) machine and enough AV technology to outfit a blockbuster film's editing room.

Berent and Weisse secured a week off every month for research and a four-day schedule, doing patient intakes and surgeries on alternate days. A lot of married couples might cringe at spending every moment together. "But we never fight at home," says Berent. "We always fight here, so we get out the frustration over the procedure." Sometimes it happens in the OR. "Our nurses all feel like they're working with Mom and Dad."

With Berent in charge of endoscopy and Weisse heading up radiology, they have a roughed-out division of labor. Weisse leads surgeries on airways and blood vessels, Berent handles digestive and urinary issues, and they split up the remainder. Often they work in tandem. But most of their procedures have one thing in common. "Our whole body is made of tubes," says Weisse. "That's kind of our bread and butter."

IR and IE are suited to vet medicine in some very specific ways. Pet inbreeding leads to all sort of disorders best dealt with interventionally rather than invasively. Snub-nosed dogs and toy breeds have airway trouble; smaller dogs and cats have urinary problems, which account for three quarters of AMC's IR/IE business. A cat that can't pee used to be either euthanized or hooked up to an external tube that had to be drained twice daily. Today, one or two stents can fix it. A bleeding kidney used to be removed—a terrible idea because often the other kidney will bleed, too—but now Berent can cauterize it with a simple injection.

The vanguard of vet medicine can also be a lot of fun.

Weisse's enthusiasm is contagious to his students; "Hey man, look at this," he'll say in front of a CT image of a dog's chest, improvising a hypothesis about concave breastbones as a contributing factor to breathing problems. Or he'll show off a newfangled pressure gauge, a Dacron-covered stent, or a 3-D-printed replica of an obstructed kidney.

Like any ambitious child of the eighties, Weisse loves the shiny toys. In addition to the classic stent—a laser-cut cylinder he likes to call "a two thousand dollar screen door"—IR surgeons work with hydraulic occluders, ameroid constrictors, coils and balloons of various kinds. During my visit, Weisse meets with a medical supplier and waxes poetic about oversized platinum coils. In their early days, Weisse and Berent used expired hardware left over from human medicine. But ultimately, says Weisse, "You want to show that this is actually profitable, this is part of your practice, you could make money. And, you know," he says as a jokey afterthought, "help animals and stuff." It works out nicely when you can play with new toys, make a tidy profit, and heal vulnerable creatures at the same time.

SOON AFTER THE MORNING rounds the animals arrive, with all their smelly real-world complications. Dignan, a wiry terrier mix, somehow pulled a stent out of her vulva, which necessitates some unseemly poking around. But the pathway is still clear, and Dignan goes home. The next visitor is much trickier. Mullet, a scraggly gray shorthair cat, is twenty years old and really showing his age. While a couple techs extract some blood, Berent sits with her intern and draws up a problem list on the back of a manila envelope: "TCC," or metastatic bladder cancer; "CKD," or chronic kidney disease; "pancreatitis; chronically hypertensive; may be blind; a history of seizures; diabetes; history of epistaxis," or nosebleeds; "and a heart murmur." Examining his fur, she points to the tenth problem. Those bumps on his neck are skin cancer—but only stage two. His case might seem depressing except for three things: he's made it to twenty in decent shape; he's under the care of two of the world's best vets; and his matrix of troubles might be fodder for groundbreaking innovations.

Berent pulls out a contrast study of Mullet's last X-ray, which highlights some injected fluid in white as it runs through two previously inserted stents. By the urethra, at the bottom of the cat, is a stent that's working just fine; the white flows straight through the urinary tract—until it stops just at the entrance to the bladder. Cancers like Mullet's grow very slowly in cats, but his tumor has pushed right through the mesh of the second, upper stent. Tomorrow they might put in a solid-material stent to clear it. The problem is that a covered stent might also block the ureters, which bring urine from the kidneys. A new uncovered stent wouldn't do that, but it may only buy them a couple of months before the tumor grows through again.

And there's another issue. "It's a really old cat," Berent says with a sigh. "The people are coming from New Hampshire. They're actually crazy. This cat is their entire world. This is their child." A few minutes later, Berent and a couple other vets walk downstairs to see the owners, already seated in one of the exam rooms behind the waiting area.

Mullet's parents seem perfectly pleasant, if a little high-strung. The woman is fond of Winnie-the-Pooh-branded accessories. She holds a small dog in her lap. The man wears what appear to be cycling pants. They are both rail-thin.

"Hi guys, you're back!" says Berent. "So I'm just going to go through all this." She's only skimmed the paperwork, she confesses to the owners; Mullet's medical rap sheet is fifty pages long. "But you feel like, other than the trips to the bathroom, he has a good quality of life?"

"I do," says the man. Up until a month ago, he explains, the stent "was amazing. He was one pee and done." But recently Mullet started going in dribs and drabs, just as he had before the procedure.

Berent shows them the X-ray and pulls out a covered stent, a flexible tube two inches long. She explains the downside; it might obstruct the ureters. Normally they could opt for a more invasive alternative called SUB—a subcutaneous urinary bypass. But at this stage, "It's risky and he doesn't need it. He's twenty."

"He's twenty and a half!" the woman says.

"We're very aware," her partner chimes in, "and we're thinking, should we just not do it?"

Berent advocates gently for the platinum standard. "If you feel like the last four months had great quality of life, then age is not his disease. *This* is his disease. So I can't say not to do it. It's like telling a ninety-year-old person they can't have a new hip. [That] they should be crippled the rest of their days and uncomfortable. So my feeling is, if you can afford it, and he has a great quality of life because of it, it's worth doing. If he doesn't, it's not."

There seems to be some disagreement on this point. "He recovered really well from the last surgery," the woman says. "Well, the recovery was hard," her partner offers. He would definitely be against the more invasive SUB, and if a covered stent blocked the ureters they'd have to do that. Maybe better to put in an uncovered stent and give Mullet another three months of peeing comfortably?

"It's hard when you have a cat who's eating, purring, happy, and you're gonna die because you can't pee," says the woman. "He's a perfectly fine cat except for this stupid tumor." She fails to mention the other nine items on Mullet's problem list. Her partner agrees, to a point. "I'm just wondering if a regular stent—"

"I'm leaving it up to you guys," says Berent. "Because we're not doing anything right now and I have eight other appointments to see." They ask her to go through the options again, and she does. "I can't be responsible," Berent concludes. "If I felt strongly I would tell you." She says she'll wait for an ultrasound on Mullet later in the day. If the ureters look clear, she'll push for a closed stent. She takes their numbers and gives them the estimate: only $3,500, because it's a second procedure. "If we wind up doing a SUB"—a last resort on the operating table—"it'll go up to ten thousand dollars. But let's hope not."

Later in the day, Berent stops by the ultrasound room, the domain of Dr. Fischetti, the same specialist who recommended string-removal surgery for Beaux the cat. Fischetti starts theorizing about Mullet's cancer but she cuts him off. "Any uretal obstruction?" "No." And off she goes. She will advise the covered stent, but the New Hampshire couple will say they prefer uncovered.

Back upstairs, Weisse is discussing Sully, a seven-month-old Bernese mountain dog. Sully probably has an intrahepatic shunt—a condition in which the portal vein, which is supposed to bring blood to the liver, bypasses it instead, slowly depriving the organ of its blood supply. "So the question is, do they want to treat this dog now," says Weisse, noting that Sully isn't full-grown yet. It's time to see the owner and find out, so we head back down to the same exam room, now occupied by a well-put-together woman in her forties and a gorgeous seventy-pound Bernese puppy.

"Cute as a button," says Weisse, giving Sully a cheerful once-over. "Mandy"—the intern on the case—"got me up to speed on everything. Is he almost eight months of age?"

"Yeah, June first." The owner says Sully's parents were small for "Berners," so he probably is almost full-grown. She absorbs all the details swiftly, and it's not too surprising when she says she's a pediatric nurse. "I always wanted to be a vet, but you know, it's just too sad. I'd rather do children."

"Everyone always says that!" says Weisse. "It's a lot like children, though. You're talking to the parents because the kids can't often say what's wrong. It's like a puzzle that you put together." He makes a face at Sully. "Right? Why do you look so surprised?" He adds that Sully looks "a little subdued, but he's in good body condition and that might be one of the most important things."

Sully is a perfect example of interventional radiology's benefits for pets of all ages—not just geriatric cases but animals with full lives ahead of them. A conventional surgery, Weisse explains to the owner, would close off the shunt (or abnormal bypass) completely, causing a blood pressure buildup in the intestines that could turn fatal. The median prognosis with regular surgery is up to two years; with IR, it's six years, and he suspects it's gotten better since their last study, based on the first one hundred cases. As with

Mullet's closed stent, the procedure is new enough that the outcome is somewhat uncertain, and every new case is a big new data point.

Weisse demonstrates all this with the help of a schematic drawing and some props. "So this is a metal tube," he says, holding up the stent. "It costs two thousand dollars, and we put it right here," he says, laying it across his rendering of the caudal vena cava, the large central vein that runs through the liver. They'll insert the stent through the jugular vein. He pulls out a gray packet of tiny coils, explaining that they will go into the shunt until they push up against the stent and start blocking blood flow—not all of it, but enough to reestablish a pressure gradient and divert blood into the liver. It's hard to say how many they'll need. "It's more of an art than a science." They cost around $50 each.

"On Wednesday afternoon," he continues, "you'll come in, you'll pick him up, he'll have a bandage on his neck. He'll look exactly the same to you and you'll wonder what you spent eight thousand dollars on. That's the typical thing that happens." But gradually—ideally—he'll become a normal, active dog. "If at any point during that transition, something goes wrong—if he looks at you funny—you call me. But we think eighty percent of these dogs will have a good long-term prognosis."

Now comes the money talk. The owner explains that

Sully's breeder refunded her half of her money when she found out about the genetic condition.

"That's all?" Weisse asks.

"Well, I think we kind of felt bad," says the owner.

"*You* felt bad? It's up to you, but taking care of this costs way more than the money back." Once they confirm the shunt via CT scan, he'll give her a report to show to the breeder as proof. A full refund would benefit the owner but also, of course, the hospital—because the owner could spend money more freely.

Weisse is reconciled to the cost of such high-end tertiary care—which is still 10 percent of the real cost of comparable human health care. "People spend money on such ridiculous stuff," he says later. "If you spend sixty thousand dollars on a car, you have a problem with someone spending that on their dog? Everyone has different values. The hardest for us is when you know someone doesn't have the money. But most of the cases we see are people that have a decent disposable income."

There are extremes, of course. Mullet and Sully are two of the four pets slotted in for procedures tomorrow. Another pet will have stem cells implanted—a cutting-edge treatment for kidney disease on a dog that would otherwise have a thirteen-day prognosis. And then there's Ferdinand, a thirteen-year-old shih tzu with advanced bladder cancer. His owners just want him to "die peeing," like Joey, the couple's first surgery together. Berent and Weisse discuss his case during afternoon rounds.

"The owners ultimately elected to do both urethral and ureteral bilateral stents," says an intern. That's one behind the penis and two near the kidneys—but no chemo and not even a cancer check.

"You can talk people into anything," Weisse teases Berent. "Except bladder surgery."

"I tried to talk about her bladder! Who was with me? I said now's the time, let's do it!" They didn't want the more radical option of bladder replacement.

"And now they want to do this," says Weisse, "for ten thousand dollars. They're cool if it's incontinent? They know the prognosis is like seventy days."

"No, I haven't talked to them about that," Berent deadpans. "I figured let them spend ten thousand dollars, who cares how long the dog lives?" She pauses for a beat. "Of course I talked to them about it! I said, 'ten thousand dollars for seventy-eight days, that's okay with you?'"

"They were totally cool?"

"Yes, and I said it could be less," says Berent. "If your dog lives for two weeks, would that be okay?"

"A week?" Weisse asks. "There must be a certain amount of days they wouldn't be happy with—like, seven and a half."

———

THE NEXT MORNING, WEISSE and Berent were already prepping poor twenty-year-old Mullet for surgery when Berent took a call from his indecisive owners. They had finally come around to a covered stent. The subsequent procedure goes well except for a last-minute bit of improvisation. The stent they planned on using is too long, so they do something they'd only done a couple of times before; they cut it in half. When a chance to improvise presents itself and it seems safe, "you go for it," says Weisse. If it works, it's an innovation.

As the team is wrapping up Mullet's procedure, Sully is already lying in the middle of the office floor, doctors and techs stepping nonchalantly around him. The Bernese is shaved from chin to nipples, a catheter poking out from a nickel-size hole in his neck. Soon two techs are placing him on the surgery table next door.

The IR surgery room feels like the set of an eighties science-fiction film. Suspended from the ceiling by a ten-foot-long beam is a white G-shaped arc. Attached to one end of it is a heavy square X-ray machine. Everyone in the room wears lead jackets with neck attachments that cover their thyroids, and Weisse wears protective goggles. A sound system softly plays Ella Fitzgerald. Between ordering up wires and clamps and saline in preparation for Sully, Weisse recalls shopping around for surgery suites. "There was one where you could actually ask the room for a compliment. I swear to God, I'm not making that up. You ask and they'd say, 'You're doing a great job today.'"

"That sounds nothing like a surgeon," quips Leo, the tech who will be operating the live X-ray (or fluoroscope) as well as three large screens suspended over the surgery table. Leo sits in a corner behind two computers, transmitting whatever video Weisse needs at the moment: reference ultrasounds, the live fluoroscopy feed, angiograms, and a camera focused on the incision—which in these kinds of surgeries is the least interesting angle.

Lasting about an hour, Sully's procedure is painstaking but never tedious. Three visitors, a resident, an intern, and two or three techs are on hand. Weisse orders up contrast dye to be shot into the veins, and uses a foot pedal to record the result. The video charts the blood flow, which he freeze-frames to outline the borders of the vessels. He feeds a guide wire in through the catheter in Sully's jugular. Superimposed on the screen is a faint ruler.

The contrast reveals a thick straight vein—the highway that is the vena cava—along with a tributary road that swoops down from the right, does a loop, and rejoins the vena cava about twenty millimeters to the left. That tributary is the shunt; it bypasses the liver and it's not supposed to exist. Today's job is not to remove it but to block off most of its traffic. Weisse uses a pressure gauge attached to the catheter to measure blood pressures at opposite ends of the vena cava. The pressures are the same; the goal is to increase the pressure gradient so that it's higher below the liver than above, forcing blood into the atrophied vessels that should be feeding the organ.

Next, Weisse uses the faint ruler to measure the length and width of the area he'll need to block off with the stent. It has to extend from the beginning of the shunt—the exit ramp off the vena cava—to the part where it rejoins the highway. Next he inserts a narrow tube through the catheter. Inside the tube (the "sheath") is a wire and, at the tip of it, the compressed stent. This one is "unreconstrainable"; once it's placed it can never be removed. There's no room for error.

A *click click click* signals that Weisse's foot is on the pedal, giving him a strobe-like video of the action—really a series of snapshots running together like a flipbook. He leads the sheath down through the vena cava and retracts the tube in the right place. The stent opens out gradually. "Just let it slide off," he says. "Like a video game, right?" The room is very quiet, except for Chet Baker on the sound system. "Is the jazz putting everybody to sleep?" he asks. "If I had that other room, I'd ask for a compliment right now."

The stent pops into place against the vessel walls. "So this is going to act as the screen door to hold the coils," says Weisse. He asks Leo for another device—a sheath that dispenses the coils. It's bent at the end, so he can guide it through turns just by twisting it. As the feed goes live again (*click click click*), the sheath drops in through one of the holes in the stent's "screen door." Slowly, a little wire emerges from the sheath and twists into a coil, which the blood flow carries up until it hits the screen door. He guides Mandy, the intern who sat with him and Sully's owner, through the insertion of a couple of coils. "Keep going, keep going," he says when she hesitates.

One after the other, the coils drop in and bunch up against the "screen door." Weisse takes over maneuvering the sheath so that coils are evenly dispersed. "Good, they're piling up nicely," he says. He measures the blood pressures, but even after ten coils, no gradient has developed. That can happen, so he isn't worried. It takes time for the coils to clot up. He stops at twenty. As he said, it's more an art than a science. I ask the visiting intern from Michigan if he sees a lot of IR work at his hospital. "What they see here in a day is what we see in a month."

"All right, wrap the neck," Weisse finally says. It's been a relatively uncomplicated procedure. Within minutes Weisse is gossiping with the visiting vets about their respective hospitals. "How many esophageal strictures do you see in a year?" he asks the Boston visitor.

"Like one or two a year probably? I've got one right now that's bad. I've ballooned it three times."

"Oh, dude," says Weisse. "You've gotta put a tube in it!"

After a quick lunch break, we're off to Ferdinand's surgery—the $10,000 triple-stent dying-dog procedure. A team effort between Weisse and Berent, it proves to be a lot more complicated than Sully.

There's no music for this one, and the difficulty ahead for the little intubated shih tzu quickly becomes evident. "He's got a very old bladder, poor guy," Berent says, pointing to a large obstruction visible on the screen. She aims the first catheter in through the penis and urethra; onscreen, it strains against the entrance into the bladder. Several times it curls back on itself. "Usually it slides right in," she says. "It's never good if you can't even get through the tumor in the urethra. Poor dog."

"Oh dear," says Weisse. "We could snare it. You have a big EN Snare, Leo?" The EN Snare is a wire that ends in four little lassos, tiny nooses that can tighten to catch the end of another wire. They had planned to run a single wire straight through the urethra and into the ureter toward the kidney, but the tumor forbids it. Instead, they'll need to puncture the kidney through an incision and run a wire into the bladder the other way, then lasso that wire with the snare from the bladder and pull it back through the urethra, creating a continuous path from kidney to penis.

Even the plan-B operation proves tricky. The kidney is rock hard, and so is the ureter. As Berent pushes the wire farther in, it hits an invisible block and goes no farther; it won't go from the ureter into the bladder. For twenty minutes, the wire curls in, like an eel bouncing off an aquarium wall. Weisse takes over to give it one last try.

"My hands are numb, I can't feel them moving," says Berent, addressing the observers across the sterile table. "We predicted that would happen, based on just how tight—"

Suddenly a murmured cheer erupts. Weisse has broken through, and the guide wire sits in the bladder.

"Excellent," says Berent. "Hold on, let me get the sheath in." She snares the guide wire and pulls it through the urethra easily. "Hold on, dog's waking up." She waits while a tech re-ups Ferdinand's anesthesia.

Now Berent needs to push another sheath into the urethra over the guide wire in order to get the far stent in. What follows feels like a highly technical version of a couple squabbling about how best to fit into a tight parking spot. "Keep going, keep going—back up for one second," Weisse says as Berent hits resistance.

"I've never not been able to get a wire through," she says. This time, it won't budge.

"Why do you keep injecting contrast?" asks Weisse.

"I have to see where the hole is," Berent answers.

"But there's no place for it to go, it won't inject," says Weisse.

"I thought we drained it."

"You're gonna overfill the system!"

The techs and interns look down at their gloves. Mommy and Daddy are fighting.

Berent pushes the sheath in again and it seems to go through. But they can't tell, in this two-dimensional rendering, whether it's in the ureter or not. Leo tilts the entire contraption to change the angle. And it's true: the sheath isn't in. It's gone through a puncture and out into who knows where.

They run a contrast, and the fluid disperses just at the spot Berent was aiming for. At some point during the procedure, they tore through the bladder. It's a tiny puncture, a harmless complication, but a sure sign that plan B won't work. "I just worry about stents in this spot at all," says Weisse. "We're gonna just bilateral SUB it. This tumor is like a rock."

Berent sighs. "The last time this happened was 2009," she explains. The rest of the surgery is fairly straightforward, if bloodier. After putting in the easiest stent, which widens the urethra just behind the penis, they open up the belly, insert catheters into the kidneys and urethra, and plug the ends into a three-way port, a cylinder that looks like a large coin. It'll be a little door just under the skin, for easy cleaning and access to urine samples. They run water through to test for leaks and, satisfied, close it up.

Weisse and Berent regard the mixed results with

equanimity—as a learning and teaching experience. What happened to them in this pristine $2.5 million facility was fairly analogous to Elisha Frye's tricky surgery in the outdoor barn. Something went wrong and, through a combination of persistence and skill and in spite of some frustration, they made it right. The patient lived another day. The cow stood back up; Ferdinand will pee again. The catastrophe of infection was averted. Next time they might do it a little differently: Frye will use less sedation; Berent will argue more strongly for a bladder replacement. Whether pushing the outer limits of pet longevity or just securing the short-term health of a milk animal, the vets persisted in the imperfect practice of helping animals live better and longer lives. The rewards and the costs look and feel so different, depending on what corner of the field a vet chooses to occupy. But the process of becoming better, day by day—savoring the triumphs, learning from the missteps, and accepting the inevitable limits—defines the mission of every veterinarian.

CONCLUSION:
ALWAYS MOVING FORWARD

Elisha Frye is out on farm calls on the day, in late 2016, when her husband, Chris, greets me in their cabin one evening. At his side is Sandy, the spry, elderly golden retriever they saved together, and dozing on his chest, oblivious to both our conversation and Chris's looming research-paper deadline, is their baby daughter, Seneca. Like Chick Weisse, another husband of a vet, Frye can't help but take his work home with him. Also like Weisse, he spends his days bringing animal medicine closer to its human equivalent. But instead of cutting-edge technology, Frye mostly imports human medicine's latest findings on prevention and fitness into animal care. Having completed Cornell's first residency in animal sports medicine and rehab—a nascent field focused on neurological health, post-surgical recovery, and geriatric fitness—he's now the new department's first assistant professor.

Like AMC's IR department, Frye often deals with animals

at their sickest. He diagnoses "unusual lameness"—like an Iranian refugee dog with a severely damaged spine, which his team rescued from paralysis over many months of physical therapy. He rehabilitates other dogs after serious surgeries using underwater treadmills, electrical stimulation, and back-leg trusses. (He also injects platelets and, just like Weisse and Berent, uses stem cells.) But in healthier dogs, Frye likes to focus on preventive health, nutrition, and above all, mobility.

"It's such an enormous part of their quality of life," says Frye. "They don't sit around and play chess and backgammon and watch TV. They need to be out and using their nose and their brain." For dogs, a decline in mobility is the first step on the slippery slope to euthanasia. The ability to get around has a big impact on quality of life for humans, but for animals it really is a matter of life or death.

There's something almost old-fashioned about Frye's apple-a-day approach to pet care, a sensibility that's partly inherited. Frye has an ancestral connection to veterinary medicine's origins in mixed-vet practice—the James Herriot–style work that his wife still practices. His great-grandfather was among Cornell's earliest veterinary graduates—class of 1914, as documented in an ancient class photo that hangs in the school's hallway. The ancestor died of undulant fever, a bovine illness treatable today with antibiotics. The younger Frye grew up communing with animals on his grandparents' New Hampshire dairy farm.

After college, Frye taught elementary-school science in New Hampshire, but soon felt the family's common calling. He took some post-bac courses, volunteered with mixed-animal vets, and got into Cornell, which is where he met Elisha. He initially leaned toward general practice, but was drawn more and more to "the science of things," as well as nutrition. So Frye kept in touch with his mentors at Cornell, and when they were looking to start a new subfield, they recruited him.

Today he splits his time between clinical work, research, and the creation of a new course in sports medicine. Once a year, he goes up to Alaska to work as a field vet during sled races, which brings out the sporty side of his job—"I love the way athletes move," he says. Closer to home, he relishes the doctor-client bond that develops over the time it takes to solve and manage difficult cases.

Frye's clients devote weeks and months to at-home therapy, investing lots of time as well as money. Like Terry, the Park City surgeon, Frye works with owners who are interested only in the highest standard of care. There aren't too many jobs where you can be a professor, field medic, family doctor, and animal wrangler at the same time. Looking back, Frye sometimes longs for private practice. "I miss the variety," he says. He's satisfied and excited about his work, but "I feel like every four years, I switch what I'm doing. Four years from now, I could be doing something completely different. I might just be that type of person."

Toward the end of my conversation with Frye—still holding his daughter, eager to get back to the research he sneaks in during baby naps—I ask him a rude question. Why copy advances in human medicine when he could be practicing it? Given that doctors make more money for something society values more highly, even though they study no harder and spend no more in tuition, why become a vet at all?

"I think all veterinarians have that chip on their shoulder," he says. "We're equally trained, and now with the veterinary specialists, we're mimicking human medicine as well." He's worn that chip, too, "but now I have a different type of insight, and maybe that has come with age. Animals give a lot, and they never ask, really, for anything back. So when we do give something back, I think that's wonderful. I believe that we're just truly privileged to have a society that supports it. I really think it's a privilege to be able to do the job I do."

It's a little jarring to hear about "privilege" in the context of a job that involves so much sweat and sacrifice. But being able to pursue a genuine passion really is a privilege. Almost all vets remember feeling at some point a sense of calling, whether it came at the age of six or crept up on them as they thought about a second or third career. At some stage of their lives, given the right opportunities and talents, an interest in science combined with a love of animals into an ambition they just couldn't shake.

"As I got older I started to contemplate what I wanted to do in the world," says Pamela Schwartz, the surgeon at AMC. "I thought about human medicine briefly but then I thought, 'Why not do it in pets?' I can have the best of both worlds—do medicine and work with creatures that I really love to be around."

The vet's ambition feeds itself, becoming more rewarding even as it grows more challenging. Schwartz wasn't the only vet to tell me that what makes the field so difficult—its variety and unpredictability—is exactly what makes it so exhilarating. "It keeps me on my toes," says Dr. Trafny, the ER vet. "I'm always learning, and I don't know what I'm walking into every day. You don't get a chance to be complacent." Dr. Cruse, the mobile-clinic freelancer, loves never having to stand still. "Every day is different, and every patient is different, and no clinic is the same," she says. Never mind those rapid-fire, hand-numbing days of spay after neuter after spay: "This is definitely not a job you get bored at. There's always an opportunity to continue growing as the field grows."

Private practitioners, meanwhile, relish the more traditional satisfaction of growing older with their patients and their clients. "I love being able to care for people's pets from beginning to end," says Johanna Ecke, the New Orleans vet. "Even with this debt burden, I really wouldn't want to do anything else."

But for those who still aren't satisfied, there's always something else on the horizon—a new technique to learn or specialty to try. For Tracy Akner, a single mother who worked for years in private practice, the job became both too harrowing and too predictable. She found a way out by chasing a personal passion: acupuncture. Akner began using it more and more in her practice as a way of dealing with cases of chronic pain and illness, until one day, tired of the constant pressure and never enamored of the ER adrenaline rush, she found a more peaceful and flexible path. She left the clinic where she worked and opened up an acupuncture business of her own. "There are people who love running around from emergency to emergency," she says. "I love to just sit with a dog for the twenty minutes that the needles are in doing *absolutely nothing*."

I asked Akner what I asked many vets: Would she recommend the profession to a young person? I got a very common answer: Absolutely, if it's what they really want. To discourage them would be to deprive them of the chance to chart their own course, just as she did. "It's really hard for me to say to someone that, because of these practical considerations, don't do what your dream is. If you're willing to be a little flexible and change your plans, you can find happiness."

Happiness—of a specifically type-A variety—is the profession's real reward. Curiosity, compassion, and the drive to solve problems are more than just mitigating factors for the stresses of being a vet; they are also the most important compensation. "I don't think I could picture anything more rewarding than what we do," says Jesse Terry. "Being able to take these dogs to surgery and see their recovery and the impact that I've made—there's a lot of easier ways to make a living, but when I drive home at the end of the day, I can't think of another profession that could offer the fulfillment of seeing how my dogs do."

There is also, for many vets, the sense of being a part of something bigger than oneself—the improbable companionship of people and animals, or even the cycle of life on Earth. "As a dairy vet, I feel like I am making a difference in the world," Elisha Frye explained to me, months after my 2016 visit. "I'm part of a chain of people providing safe meat and milk for the country, and I'm helping people with their livelihood. So after completing a challenging day, I go home with a lot of job satisfaction." And now that winter was long past, she felt compelled to add: "A beautiful spring day helps a lot, too."

CHANGING SEASONS CAN CHANGE your perspective, and so can new circumstances. When I checked in again with

Frye more than a year later, things looked very different. The Fryes had just had their second child, and Elisha had realized, as many female farm vets do, that it was time to reassess her career. So she left Midstate and farm animals behind. Frye had always been excellent at interpreting test results; now she puts those skills to use as a consultant with the Cornell-affiliated New York State Animal Diagnostic Lab. She helps formulate checklists, read results, and monitor herd and human health for state regulators.

"I literary don't touch animals anymore," she reports, "unless they're dead already." (She adds that Sandy is still very much alive—pushing seventeen.) "Weird, huh? For me, it was the right time. A few years ago, I wouldn't have been ready to leave the field."

So it goes for many members of an occupation where change is becoming the status quo. Happiness can be found in trying out a new specialty; in moving to a new city; in knowing when to move on. James Herriot visions notwithstanding, the most satisfied vets I talked to didn't simply set up a shingle and wait for bliss to arrive. They got it wrong on the first or second or fourth job, and kept trying.

Several months after showing me around her practice, Catherine Wood left All Creatures Veterinary Hospital. She and her partner were simply not compatible. She continues doing shift work in New York and Maryland, and she travels frequently to animal sanctuaries in Africa. Her passion is wildlife medicine, and one day she'll find a way to practice it full-time.

Throughout Michael Lund's tenure at the ASPCA, he kept one eye on his career as a manager and another on pathology. "If school's in the cards, I'll take it," he said after his first round of residency rejections. "If I'm not accepted a few more times, at some point I'm going to move on. Sometimes I think about being back out west."

But he made the most of his time at the ASPCA, leading an expansion of the mobile care program into stationary centers. When a pet owner asked him what he liked most about his field, "I looked straight at the client and reminded him that it's people like them who keep me doing what I do—the loving families that I help to better take care of their pets. It's at the center of my existence."

And then, in 2018, Michael Lund was accepted into a pathology program at the University of Pennsylvania. He got married that May and, a few months later, was in Philadelphia, learning again.

"I'm growing in new ways as a resident," he wrote to me recently. "Some days I feel more connected to my days as a clinician, but I know this decision is a wise one, regarding my own self-preservation." He's learned to see burnout on the horizon, to head it off by plotting a new course.

"My previous work experiences had definite ceilings," he continued. But now, "I'm excited to be growing in a field where the sky isn't even the limit—and the expectation is the learning will be lifelong." He still hopes to volunteer at local shelters, pull shifts in general practice, and help friends with their pets. But pathology will allow him to think bigger about animal health, to use and expand on everything he's learned in farm medicine, nonprofit care, and private practice—and to imagine that his research might change the world. "To dream is to be alive," he wrote. "I'm dreaming again and it feels pretty damn good."

After all he'd been through, I couldn't help asking Lund The Question: Would he advise a vet career for a young person? He echoed Akner and Terry: Do it for the right reasons, with passion but with open eyes. Be aware that there will be moments of doubt, exhaustion, and restlessness, and know that there is no single way to be a vet. "When you graduate, you will change," he wrote. "My story is a testament to that. You're going to try something new."

ADDITIONAL RESOURCES

It takes more than one short book to capture the breadth of the veterinary experience, so varied among specialties and, even, within them, from one day to the next. Many of the accounts below are memoirs of a sort, diverse in tone and intended audience, but each illuminates crucial areas in a vast field.

Additional Reading

All Creatures Great and Small (1972)
    By James Herriot
The Yorkshire country doctor (given name James Alfred Wight) gathered his earliest semiautobiographical tales in this collection, which branded a bucolic portrait of the village vet into the collective consciousness even as the profession was moving toward a more mechanized and professionalized mode of medicine. Yet it remains critical, colorful reading for understanding the essence and evolution of the job.

The Rhino with Glue-on Shoes: And Other Surprising True
   Stories of Zoo Vets and Their Patients (2008)
   Edited by Lucy H. Spelman and Ted Y. Mashima
Two DVMs have surveyed the globe and returned with twenty-
eight stories of wild-animal vets rescuing some of the planet's
most vulnerable creatures—from the titular Asian rhinoceros,
with his orthopedic implants, to an orphaned whale and a whole
herd of bison. Each lively case study ends with a bio of the vet,
humanizing the doctors as well as the animals.

All My Patients Have Tales: Favorite Stories from a
   Vet's Practice (2006)
   By Jeff Wells
A Colorado mixed-animal vet's breezy but economical account
provides the modern analogue to Herriot. Skipping from cows
to dogs to horses, Wells shapes his anecdotes around common-
sense information about the vet's progress through the world.

Tell Me Where It Hurts: A Day of Humor, Healing, and Hope in
   My Life as an Animal Surgeon (2008)
   By Nick Trout
For deeper insights into what vet medicine is like on the modern
frontier, Trout's twenty-four-hour tour through Angell Animal
Medical Center in Boston—a place not unlike AMC in Manhattan—is close to essential reading. Organ transplants, cancer
treatments, and even pet cosmetic surgery come in for observa-
tion and scrutiny, empathy and analysis, all in a day's work.

Gorillas in the Mist (1983)

> By Dian Fossey

Perhaps the most popular and powerful book on human devotion to animals, this one is a bit of a cheat—Fossey was a biologist and not a vet—but her description of thirteen years spent studying, living with, and defending endangered gorillas (she was later murdered by poachers) probes deeply into what connects us to other animals.

Communal Websites

A growing but relatively small group of professionals needs places to learn, improve, and commiserate. A handful of blogs and sites provide much-needed information, conversation, and solidarity.

FOR PROFESSIONALS

DVM360. The field's top magazine—targeted and practical but accessible to the general-interest reader—maintains a comprehensive website and a news page with a variety of features, from urgent stories on outbreaks and breakthroughs to lifestyle features and columns.

www.dvm360.com

Pet MD. A clearinghouse for vet information of all kinds, organized around clear tabs, includes an encyclopedia of animal conditions categorized by animal; verticals on nutrition, tools of care, and emergency checklists; and a blog given over to a rotating crew of informed practitioners.

www.petmd.com

Veterinary Information Network. This one's for the pros, built on the idea of vets helping one another in their daily clinical work, enabled by the latest technology. (In fact, the VIN network was founded in 1990 on an early precursor to AOL.) Members can access any specialist with a minute of spare time, along with neat data visualizations and demos and a board of helpful "faculty."

www.vin.com

VETgirl. Dr Justine Lee's site is a portal to her paid continuing-education webinars and podcasts, but timely discussions populate the front page, along with chatty blog posts—cheerful but always clear-eyed—on subjects ranging from how to remove fishhooks and navigate animal opioids to "life hacks" for new graduates.

www.vetgirlontherun.com

Dr. Andy Roark. A little less voicey than VETgirl, the popular YouTube vet's site (which also offers premium videos) hosts a bulletin board on many topics. There are seasonal posts "Top-Five Fourth of July Emergencies," discussions of pressing issues like the rural-vet crisis, as well as silly video memes vets need to make it through the hard days.

www.drandyroark.com

FOR STUDENTS

How I Got Into Veterinary School. The book you're reading captures only a small slice of the vet-school experience. This growing project provides plentiful resources (and links to scholarships), but its focus is a compilation of interviews with vets who had unique or instructive paths into school.

www.howigotintoveterinaryschool.com

PAWS. The startup project of a fourth-year vet student at UC Davis, short for "Pre-Vet Advising Website & Support," is fun and encouraging but information-rich, meant for vet-curious students looking to get a leg up in college—or even earlier.

www.pawsiblepaws.weebly.com

Animal Jobs Digest. Of all the prerequisites for being admitted into vet school, the hardest to figure out is hands-on pre-vet experience. This site makes it a little easier by listing positions at all levels for people who love animals but aren't necessarily medically trained.

www.animaljobsdigest.com

PROFESSIONAL ASSOCIATIONS AND
OFFICIAL ONLINE RESOURCES

Over the last couple of decades, vet work has grown increasingly diverse, but also more harrowing to navigate. Thankfully, a few interrelated professional organizations have stayed on top of the changes, not only running the system efficiently but also conducting and collecting research as a semipublic service. Here are their crucial home pages.

American Veterinary Medication Association (AVMA). A one-stop shop for veterinary support, information, research, and education, the AVMA is a professional association, founded in 1863, whose membership of 91,000 comprises almost all American vets. Its Council on Education is also in charge of accrediting all schools. Outside visitors have access to overviews of all its processes and discussions of "hot issues," while members can find studies, jobs listings, networking opportunities, and, of course, financial planning tools.

www.avma.org

Association of American Veterinary Medical Colleges (AAVMC). Once a loosely organized collection of college deans working closely with the AVMA, the AAVMC branched off in 1966 to become a nonprofit. Its website now houses all resources for applying to vet school, from a list of prerequisites required by each institution to a unified application site known as the Veterinary Medical College Application Service (VMCAS). For a more old-school resource, follow links to purchase the group's annual book, *Veterinary Medical School Admissions Requirements* (Purdue University Press).

www.aavmc.org

Veterinary Internship & Residency Matching Program. Run by the American Association of Veterinary Clinicians (AAVC), this is your portal into the streamlined process of applying to, and hopefully matching with, the internship or specialist residency of your choice. Studies and statistics are also included.

www.virmp.org

ACKNOWLEDGMENTS

This book, written within tight parameters of time and space, would simply not have come together without a handful of relatively far-flung veterinarians who decided, independently, to open up their offices and their lives to me on short notice. These are very busy professionals in stressful environments whose work does not benefit from having a nosy and ignorant interloper around, even for a few precious hours. Thanks to Chris and Elisha Frye and Elisha's former employers at Midstate Veterinary Services, especially Ken Osborn. At the Animal Medical Center in Manhattan, thanks to Jennifer Petrisko for throwing open the doors and recommending a visit to Allyson Berent and Chick Weisse in the amazing Department of Interventional Radiology and Endoscopy. Thanks as well to all the dedicated and talented doctors in AMC's department of Emergency and Critical Care. I'm grateful to Catherine Wood and Njeri Cruse, two more veterinarians who had no free time to give, but gave it anyway. Without Michael Lund's open heart, searching soul, and generous perspective, the big picture would have remained, for me, out of view. And greatest thanks of all to Robin, my sister, whose dedication to this profession of great costs and ineffable rewards inspired me to see it for myself.

ABOUT THE AUTHOR

Boris Kachka is the author of *Hothouse: The Art of Survival and the Survival of Art at America's Most Celebrated Publishing House*, which was a finalist for the National Book Critics Circle's John Leonard Prize. He has contributed essays to *Made in Russia: Unsung Icons of Soviet Design* and *Reinier Gerritsen: The Last Book*. He is currently the books editor at New York Media, where he has written about the arts and cultural institutions for many years. He has contributed to the *New York Times*, *T* magazine, *GQ*, *Elle*, *Slate*, *Salon*, and *Condé Nast Traveler*. He lives in Brooklyn, New York.